Your Seeds of Greatness

The World's Greatest Team Leadership Quote Book

By:

Michael K. Simpson

Introduction

One of the greatest quests is to live a life of greatness—one of meaning, sacrifice, and contribution.

This book is dedicated to helping unleash the greatness that already exists within every person. No matter how old or young, no matter the station in life, every person harbors a desire to be great—to reach new heights, to improve their station in life, and to make a significant difference. Some have a clear vision of who they are and what they can accomplish, while others may be wading through fear, lack of direction, disappointment, and despair. Even those who are suffering through severe trials and difficulties can do so with greatness and can eventually break through life's set-backs and become the person they are destined to be.

These insightful quotes cover many centuries, countries, and philosophies. But at its core the premise is –all great wisdom literature is based on timeless, universal, and self-evident principles that have endured throughout the ages.

The journey for capturing these quotes help us to understand that no matter how culturally, ethnically, and geographically diverse we may be, as a part of a global family – we all have common interests, needs, aspirations, and dreams to pursue. As Dr. William Fulbright stated, "We live in a world of diversity and the aim of international education is neither to convert nor to indoctrinate but to influence others with empathy and understanding."

Greatness lies like a seed within us. Some seeds are planted in fertile, nutrient-dense soil and are apt to yield a bountiful harvest, while other seeds lie in what seem to be barren fields of rocks and noxious weeds. These undeveloped seeds can also provide great results; however, they need to be watered, cultivated, nurtured, and prepared to blossom.

With regard to the influence of people around us, I like what Mahatma Gandhi stated: "It takes a village to raise a family." We have all had people in our lives who inspire and lift us to greater heights—spouses, parents, siblings, family members, friends, teachers, bosses, mentors, colleagues, spiritual leaders, athletic coaches, and political leaders. Looking at them, we realize that there is no greater role than that of being an inspiring leader to others. We all know people who have helped us accomplish great things in life. Often they are the ones who saw and uncovered the small seeds of greatness or latent potential that lies within each of us. In my professional career, I have learned and worked with many of the great ones, some of the brightest and most influential leaders in business, government, and academia. It has been an amazing blessing and privilege to learn and access information from such inspiring and diverse races, ethnicities, cultures, and traditions, including: Muslim, Hindu, Sikh, Confucian,

Buddhist, Judaism, Christian, Atheist, and many others. In all of my coaching and consulting work, "the seeds of greatness" have been found virtually everywhere on the planet.

More specifically, my work has been focused on helping others clarify and develop individual, team and company purpose, vision, strategy, goal execution, leadership capability, and in unleashing their talent among managers and teams.

Many of these quotes have been a great help in my leadership training, work sessions, seminars, and keynote speeches, as well as in coaching sessions. In my work, I have observed leaders, managers, and teams who lack passion, are unfocused, stressed, burned out, imbalanced, fatigued, uninspired, disconnected, disengaged, and ambivalent about how they can truly make a difference at home or at work. Despite losing sight of one's true nature and reason for being, I truly believe everyone wants to be great and make a difference in life. I believe all people genuinely want to be inspired, connected to a real purpose, to add meaning, expand their influence, and make a significant contribution. In short, they want to unlock the greatness that is within themselves, their teams, and their organizations.

In life, we may have personally experienced great limitations, weaknesses, disappointments, trials, and failures. Don't let fear, set-backs, procrastination, victimization, or discouragement define who you are. Be persistent, as lasting change never happens over-night. With each new day comes a fresh start, full of hope and opportunity to get better. Even though we may fall short of our finish line, the journey of becoming and striving to be better will raise your motivation and performance at higher levels success that you ever thought possible. E. Stanley Jones insights help to support this point of view, "Why not trust your hopes instead of your fears? When you do, you will think optimistically about yourself and your world…and then you will begin to share that optimism with others. They'll be better for it, and so will you." Many cultures have the tradition and practice of making New Year's resolutions. Setting goals is an very important endeavor to help motivate, stretch, and improve our lives. Setting goals can bring out the best that is within us. Actually keeping and sustaining goals is another thing. It has been said that it takes 21 days to change a habit. Therefore, the challenge for "Your Seeds of Greatness" is to review and study these quotes, identify personally opportunities that motivate and inspire you, then, seek to set realistic and achievable goals that will improve your life, important relationships, work, and the best that is within others.

While doing research on this project, I partnered with a fellow colleague Dr. David Paxman and an intern named Luke Ball. We reviewed, scanned, and organized literally thousands and thousands of quotes from a vast number of books, articles, journals, speeches, and literature reviews. In doing so, it was humbling to tap into some of the greatest thinkers and minds who have lived on this earth. As we organized these ideas and quotes in these books, we realized how blessed we were to have access to an abundance of great truths and ideas that lift the soul. This book is dedicated to my wife, my family, and future generations that may benefit from these inspiring ideas. My desired is to positively impact all of the people, cultures, and ethnicities that have inspired me. Many of the quotes represent thought-provoking ideas and timeless principles that are just as practical today, as when they were uttered decades and even centuries before.

As I reflect on these organized quotes, I have confirmed another piece of wisdom: every dream, aspiration, strategy, goal, and resolution needs to involve the right mindset, motive, morals and ethics that are aligned to improve personal behaviors. Whether an individual leader seeks to engage their team; align their organizational resources, systems and structures; or build a life and family that serve and contribute to the larger social environment, I believe that all people's lives are interconnected. Therefore, this book is organized around these four integral aspects of life:

1. Personal Leadership
2. Team Engagement
3. Organization Alignment
4. Family/Society Contribution

Thus, within each aspect of life, the reader will find strands that connect the personal to the team, the organization to the personal, and the family to the social. As Mahatma Gandhi put it so clearly, "My life is an indivisible whole, and all my activities run into one another...my life is my message."

May this book of inspirational quotes and wisdom literature inspire you, your families, your teams, and your organizations to help to uncover and unlock Your Seeds of Greatness. May you find your own vision, hope, passion, talent, and contribution that will guide you on your exciting and successful journey through life. On your journey in life, remember to seek to bless and uplift all of those around you and to follow Sir Winston Churchill's advice, "Never, never, never give up!"

Best of happiness and success!

Michael K. Simpson

Author Acknowledgments

In my career, I have traveled throughout the world conducting leadership work sessions, keynote speeches, consulting in strategy execution, training in talent management, and offer executive coaching approximately two-hundred plus days per year. The travel has been intense but the work is unbelievably fulfilling and rewarding. I have learned more from my clients than they ever could learn from me. On this journey, I have enjoyed seeking to influence the influential in people, teams, and organizations everywhere!

During my travels, I have had free time to research, read, and write on airplanes, in airports, and hotel rooms. Therefore, it seemed natural that a book project like this would be both fun and inspiring to pursue while offering great value to clients and society at large. After four years of personally compiling many of the world's best quotes, I realized this project was way too big to be done alone. I partnered with an intelligent and insightful retired professor of English literature, Dr. Paxman. He helped to organize quotes by subject and content category and by a series of powerful and provocative questions. This addition was brilliant because it offers all readers the ability to easily access to a mass amount of content by topic area. Our guiding principle with this book is that there is plenty of information in the world – the key is to make it easy to access and simple to use. I would also like to thank my intern Luke Ball who was an undergraduate business strategy student in BYU's Marriott School of Management. Luke worked tirelessly for over two semesters reviewing, researching, inputting, and organizing thousands of quotes from boxes and boxes of compiled books, journals, magazines, articles, and speeches.

Anne Bruns, offered insights as an experienced editor from a local Utah publishing company. She leveraged her skills in editing, referencing, citations, and ongoing reviews. Her input proved to be very detailed and professional.

Lastly, the entire quote book was transformed into an eBook format for easy access of content online and for mass digital distribution. Zach Kristensen, CEO of Juxtabook Digital Marketing, used his expertise to design and format the eBook. He spent countless hours reviewing and organizing all of our content. His experience made these quotes digitally compatible to read, distribute, promote, and sell in eBook, enhanced eBook, and print on demand, and smart phone application formats. To learn how to use Zach's services for putting content or books into an eBook format, please contact him at www.juxtabook.com or 801-410-0229.

Table of Contents

Part 2.
Team Greatness

What Kind of Team Member Am I?

The Personal Dimension

Team work and team building are largely interpersonal matters. They grow out of individual personal attributes that can't be faked for long. However, they reach out to include other people—how we see them, trust them, empower them, motivate them, and lead them.

Whether you are flying the Atlantic, selling sausages, building a skyscraper, driving a truck, or painting a picture, your greatest power comes from the fact that you want tremendously to do that very thing well. And a thing well done usually works out to the benefit of others as well as yourself. This applies to sport, business, friendships.

Amelia Earhart, *American Magazine*

❖ ❖ ❖

For most people, there's a big difference between work and play. Work is something you have to do; play is something you choose to do. I believe the greatest job is when you can't tell the difference, and the best leaders are those who absolutely love what they're doing. As Confucius said, "Choose work you love and you will never have to work a day in your life.

Ken Blanchard, *The Heart of a Leader*

❖ ❖ ❖

Do I Understand the Importance of Teams in Today's Businesses?

In any situation requiring the real-time combination of multiple skills, experiences, and judgments, a team inevitably gets better results than a collection of individuals operating within confined job roles and responsibilities. Teams are more flexible than larger organizational groupings because they can be more quickly assembled, deployed, refocused, and disbanded, usually in ways that enhance rather than disrupt more permanent structures and processes. Teams are more productive than groups that have no clear performance objectives because their members are committed to deliver tangible performance results. Teams and performance are an unbeatable combination.

Jon R. Katzenbach and Douglas K. Smith,
"The Wisdom of Teams", *Harper Business*, 1993

❖ ❖ ❖

A large group set out to climb Mt. Everest. Their unprecedented goal was to help a blind man, Erik Weihenmayer, reach the summit and return safely to base camp. The team carefully planned the route to the top of the world's tallest peak. At the end of each day, they huddled together in what they called the "tent meeting" to talk out what they had accomplished and what they had learned, which would help them plan the action for the next day. Faster climbers on the team cleared the path of obstacles and then worked their way back to meet Erik along the trail. Erik said, "Our team stuck together and took care of each other, which gave me just enough courage to finish." This cadence of accountability was the key to successful execution of the goal. On May 25, 2001, Erik Weihenmayer became the first blind person to stand on the summit of Mt. Everest. His team's other remarkable accomplishment: they had the most people from one team to reach the top of Everest in a single day.

J. Krakauer, *Into Thin Air*, 1999; Erik Weihenmayer,
Touch the Top of the World, 2002

❖ ❖ ❖

When you have been a member of a high performing team in your career, you know how the team sacrificed, felt, achieved, and performed, you fantasize throughout your entire career how you can re-create that same high level of performance again.

Katzenbach and Smith, *The Wisdom of Teams*

❖ ❖ ❖

Do I Clearly Understand the Team's
Purposes and Specific Goals?

Teams need to know why they exist, and they need to plainly see that their performance has a direct impact on the overall performance of their function, division, business unit, company, and customers. A mission is the best vehicle for answering the question "why do we exist?" and communicating to team members and others the reason the team was established.

Paula Chronister and Tig Williams, *Creating Better Teams: Five Dimensions of Designing, Implementing, and Sustaining Effective Teams,* 1996

❖ ❖ ❖

Knowledge is power they say. Knowledge is not only power it is good fun.

E.M. Forster, "Commonplace Book",
The Manager's Book of Quotations

❖ ❖ ❖

If you don't know where you are going, you'll end up someplace else.

Yogi Berra

❖ ❖ ❖

Our plans miscarry because they have no aim. When a man does not know what harbor he is making for, no wind is the right wind.

Seneca

❖ ❖ ❖

Management by objectives works if you first think through your objectives. Ninety percent of the time you haven't.

Peter Drucker

❖ ❖ ❖

The indispensable first step to getting the things you want out of life is this: decide what you want.

Ben Stein

❖ ❖ ❖

Ownership: Do I Believe in Myself and My Team?

Teams need to know which decision they are responsible for and which they are not. The more teams have ownership over the day-to-day decision affecting the task at hand, the more they can produce the expected business results.

Paula Chronister and Tig Williams, *Creating Better Teams: Five Dimensions of Designing, Implementing, and Sustaining Effective Teams*, 1996

❖ ❖ ❖

No group ever becomes a team until it can hold itself accountable as a team.

Jon R. Katzenbach and Douglas K. Smith,
"The Wisdom of Teams", *Harper Business,* 1993

❖ ❖ ❖

If we did what we are capable of doing, we would literally astound ourselves.

Ralph Waldo Emerson

❖ ❖ ❖

The best discipline, maybe the only discipline that really works, is self-discipline.

Walter Kiechel III, *Fortune Magazine*

❖ ❖ ❖

People who get ahead are those who prove they can get things done.

David Kearns

❖ ❖ ❖

The future has several names. For the weak, it is the impossible. For the fainthearted, it is the unknown. For the thoughtful and the valiant, it is ideal.

Victor Hugo

❖ ❖ ❖

The country is full of good coaches. What it takes to win is a bunch of interested players.

Don Coryell

❖ ❖ ❖

Try to be one of the people on whom nothing is lost.

Henry James, *If Ignorance Is Bliss, Why Aren't There More Happy People?*

❖ ❖ ❖

None of us is as smart as all of us.

Ken Blanchard

❖ ❖ ❖

Talent wins games, but teamwork and intelligence win championships.

Michael Jordan

❖ ❖ ❖

Coming together is a beginning. Keeping together is progress.
Working together is success.

Henry Ford

❖ ❖ ❖

Individual commitment to a group effort—that is what makes a team work, a
company work, a society work, a civilization work.

Vince Lombardi

❖ ❖ ❖

The most creative and productive work comes when people freely make
commitments to one another, not when bosses tell them what to do.

Jim Collins, *Good to Great*

❖ ❖ ❖

Stop and think about it for a minute. What do the right people want more than
almost anything else? They want to be part of a winning team. They want to
contribute to producing visible, tangible results. They want to feel the excitement
of being involved in something *that just flat-out works.* When the right people see
a simple plan born of confronting the brutal facts—a plan developed from
understanding, not bravado—they are likely to say, "That'll work. Count me in."
When they see the monolithic unity of the executive team behind the simple plan
and the selfless, dedicated qualities of Level 5 leadership, they'll drop their
cynicism. When people begin to feel the magic of momentum—when they begin
to see tangible results, when they can *feel* the flywheel beginning to build
speed—*that's* when the bulk of people line up to throw their shoulders against
the wheel and push.

Jim Collins, *Good To Great*

❖ ❖ ❖

Am I an Honest, Candid, and Transparent Team Member?

To get people that believe in honesty and candor you have to reward it, praise it, and model it—it has to be part of your core values and performance appraisals.

Jack Welch

❖ ❖ ❖

Advice is like snow; the softer it falls, the longer it dwells upon, and the deeper it sinks into the mind.

Samuel Taylor Coleridge

❖ ❖ ❖

"Inside out" means to start first with the self; even more fundamentally, to start with the most inside part of self—with your paradigms, your character, and your motives.

Stephen R. Covey

❖ ❖ ❖

Keep your promise. Surely it will be inquired into.

Surah 17: Ayah 34

❖ ❖ ❖

Our capacity to be vulnerable is not our weakness but our strength; for out of pain is born joy; and from despair, hope; and from being hated, love! To be spiritual is to be vulnerable.

Matthew Fox, *The Yearbook of Love and Wisdom*

❖ ❖ ❖

Honest criticism is hard to take—especially when it comes from a relative, a friend, an acquaintance, or a stranger.

Franklin P. Jones

❖ ❖ ❖

Critics can't even make music by rubbing their back legs together.

Mel Brooks

❖ ❖ ❖

Pay no attention to what critics say. A statue has never been erected in honor of a critic.

Jean Sibelius

❖ ❖ ❖

Before you criticize someone, walk a mile in their shoes. That way, if they get angry with you, you'll be a mile away and they'll be barefoot.

Sarah Jackson

❖ ❖ ❖

Forget about how you talk to your customers, if we cannot be honest within our management teams and have absolute candor and transparent—we will eventually fail.

Jack Welch, *Winning*

❖ ❖ ❖

In our most reflective moments, each of us wants to make a difference—a contribution. Call it a cause or call it a mission, we want [to] be a part of something meaningful. Detecting what our contribution will be on a daily basis, however, is not always easy, especially when we are so tangled up with the little things of life. Yet there comes a point when each individual should strive to clarify what he or she will stand for and what purposes he or she will choose to pursue.

Stephen R. Covey, *Everyday Greatness*

❖ ❖ ❖

To be handcuffed by a lie is the worst form of all imprisonments. May the God of all truth, lead you to truth and may the truth set you free.

Ravi Zacharias

❖ ❖ ❖

A rumor without a leg to stand on will get around some other way.

John Tudor, *Everyday Greatness*

❖ ❖ ❖

The prime occupational hazard of the manager is superficiality.

Henry Mintzberg, "The Nature of Managerial Work", *The Manager's Book of Quotations*

❖ ❖ ❖

The good-to-great leaders did not pursue an expedient "try a lot of people and keep who works" model of management. Instead they adopt the following approach: "Let's take the time to make rigorous A+ selections right up front. If we get it right, we'll do everything we can to try to keep them on board for a long time. If we make a mistake, then we'll confront the fact so that we can get on with our work and they can get on with their lives." … Said Mockler, "Every minute devoted to putting the proper person in the proper slot is worth weeks of time later."

Jim Collins, *Good To Great*

❖ ❖ ❖

Honesty is a striking feature of the relationship between self-development and integrity. People who are good at self-development have the ability to evaluate their strengths and weaknesses honestly and to acknowledge their strengths in behavior A and that they are less effective in behavior B.

John H. Zenger and Joseph Folkman, *The Extraordinary Leader*

❖ ❖ ❖

A great rule for doing business today is: Think more about your people, and they will think more of themselves. And don't act like you are perfect. Leaders need to come from behind their curtains of infallibility, power, and control, and let their "very good" side—their humanity—be revealed. Folks like to be around a person who is willing to admit his or her vulnerability, asks for ideas, and can let others be in the spotlight.

Ken Blanchard, *The Heart of a Leader*

❖ ❖ ❖

A good mind is lord of a kingdom.

Seneca, *Thoughts On Leadership*

❖ ❖ ❖

If you tell the truth you don't have to remember anything.

Mark Twain

❖ ❖ ❖

Power is actualized only when word and deed have not parted company.

Hannah Arendt

❖ ❖ ❖

Our analysis on the competency companions to teamwork revealed that having trusting relationships is strongly associated with good teamwork. That makes sense. Most relationships depend on trust as a basis for the relationship. Teams without trust suffer from conflicts and competition between team members. It is easy to talk about trust, but it tends to be an elusive quality for many leaders. To understand better the real meaning of trust, we did an analysis to determine its competency companions. Those leaders who were trusted also had the following characteristics:

Consideration for others

An open, friendly style

Noncompetitive

Others have confidence in the leader's abilities and knowledge

Careful listening

Candor

John H. Zenger and Joseph Folkman, The Extraordinary Leader

❖ ❖ ❖

In looking for people to hire, you look for three qualities: integrity, intelligence, and energy. And if they don't have the first, the other two will kill you.

Warren Buffet

❖ ❖ ❖

No legacy is so rich as honesty.

William Shakespeare

❖ ❖ ❖

You can fool some of the people all of the time, and all of the people some of the time, but you cannot fool all the people all the time.

Abraham Lincoln

❖ ❖ ❖

Never apologize for showing feeling. When you do so, you apologize for the Truth.

Benjamin Disraeli

❖ ❖ ❖

When in doubt, tell the Truth.

Mark Twain

❖ ❖ ❖

A half Truth is a whole lie.

Yiddish Proverb

❖ ❖ ❖

Those who think it is permissible to tell white lies soon grow color-blind.

Austin O'Mally

❖ ❖ ❖

A lie has speed, but Truth has endurance.

Edgar J. Mohn

❖ ❖ ❖

We tell lies when we are afraid….afraid of what we don't know, afraid of what others will think, afraid of what will be found out about us. But every time we tell a lie, the thing that we fear grows stronger.

Tad Williams

❖ ❖ ❖

Honesty is the first chapter in the book of wisdom.

Thomas Jefferson

❖ ❖ ❖

The Truth needs no rehearsal.

Barbara Kingsolver

❖ ❖ ❖

Do I Plan, Prioritize, and Manage Time Effectively?

Only 20% of workers' time is spent on tasks directly related to the organization's mission, goals, and critical objectives.

Wirthland Worldwide Research

❖ ❖ ❖

Does thou love life? Then do not squander time, for that's the stuff life is made of.

Benjamin Franklin

❖ ❖ ❖

In preparing for battle I have always found that plans are useless, but planning is indispensable.

Dwight D. Eisenhower

❖ ❖ ❖

Before everything else, getting ready is the secret of success.

Henry Ford

❖ ❖ ❖

What the heart cherishes, there its home will be.

Author Unknown

❖ ❖ ❖

Things which matter most must never be at the mercy of things which matter least.

Johann Goethe

❖ ❖ ❖

I've been on a calendar, but I've never been on time.

Marilyn Monroe

❖ ❖ ❖

Human beings are hard wired to do one thing at a time with excellence.

Jim Stuart

❖ ❖ ❖

It is not enough to stay busy. So, too, are the ants.
The question is what are you busy about?

Henry David Thoreau

❖ ❖ ❖

The nicest thing about not planning is that failure comes as a complete surprise
rather than being preceded by a period of worry and depression.

Sir John Harvey Jones, *Execution Essentials*

❖ ❖ ❖

Half our life is spent trying to find something to do with the time we have rushed
through life trying to save.

Will Rogers

❖ ❖ ❖

One of the goals of life is to try and be in touch with one's most personal
themes—the values, ideas, styles, colors that are the touchstones of one's own
individual life, its real texture, and substance.

Gloria Vanderbilt

❖ ❖ ❖

We must decide what is really important, really necessary, make it a priority, and
make time. Otherwise the siren call of the world will always keep us busy and
distracted from what really is important. What really counts?

Matthew Keely

❖ ❖ ❖

There is a time for everything, and a season for every activity under heaven.

Ecclesiastes 3:1

❖ ❖ ❖

See that all things should be done in wisdom and in order.

Mosiah 4:27

❖ ❖ ❖

Make the best use of your time, despite all the difficulties of these days.

Ecclesiasates 5:16

❖ ❖ ❖

Those who define truth by a calendar run afoul of Him who created time.

Ravi Zacharias

❖ ❖ ❖

A leader who says 'I've got ten priorities' doesn't know what he is talking about. He doesn't know himself what the most important things are. You've got to have a few, clear realistic goals and priorities...

Larry Bossidy & Ram Charan, *Execution: The Discipline of Getting Things Done*, 2002

❖ ❖ ❖

It is easy to say NO to the unimportant, no matter how urgent it is, when you have a clear sense of your mission and key goals.

Stephen R. Covey

❖ ❖ ❖

How can time argue with eternity?

Ravi Zacharias

❖ ❖ ❖

To do a job effectively, one must set priorities. Too many people let their 'in' basket set their priorities. On any given day, unimportant but interesting trivia pass through an office; one must not permit these to monopolize [your] time.

Admiral Hyman G. Rickover, "Father of the Nuclear Navy," speech, Columbia University, 1982

❖ ❖ ❖

The enemy of the great is the good. Each manager or leader never has a limit to all of the good things they can measure or go after. Our choices are mostly not between good and bad—they for each of us to distinguish between good and great.

Jim Collins, *Good to Great*

❖ ❖ ❖

It is the mark of great people to treat important matters as important and trivial matters as trivialities.

Doris Lessing

❖ ❖ ❖

The only difference between a rich person and a poor person
is how they use their time.

Robert Kiyosaki

❖ ❖ ❖

Besides the noble art of getting things done, there is the noble art of leaving
things undone. The wisdom of life consists in the elimination of non-essentials.

Lin Yutang, *Everyday Greatness,* by Stephen R. Covey

❖ ❖ ❖

The measure of success is not whether you have a tough problem to deal with,
but whether it is the same problem you had last year.

John Foster Dulles, *The 21 Indispensable Qualities of a Leader*

❖ ❖ ❖

Dost thou love life, then do not squander time, for that's the stuff life is made of.

Benjamin Franklin

❖ ❖ ❖

You will never "find" time for anything. If you want time, you must make it.

Charles Bruxton

❖ ❖ ❖

I recommend you take care of the minutes and the hours will
take care of themselves.

Earl of Chesterfield

❖ ❖ ❖

To comprehend a man's life, it is necessary to know not merely what he does but
also what he purposely leaves undone. There is a limit to the work that can be got
out of a human body or a human brain, and he is a wise man who wastes no
energy on pursuits for which he is not fitted; and he is till wiser who, from among
the things that he can do well, chooses and resolutely follows the best.

John Hall Gladstone

❖ ❖ ❖

Time is money.

Benjamin Franklin

❖ ❖ ❖

The more business a man has to do, the more he is able to accomplish,
for he learns to economize his time.

Sir Matthew Hale

❖ ❖ ❖

What people say, what people do, and what they say
they do are entirely different things.

Margaret Meade

❖ ❖ ❖

The great mystery isn't that people do things badly but that they occasionally
do a few things well. The only thing that is universal is incompetence.
Strength is always specific! Nobody ever commented, for example, that the
great violinist Jascha Heifetz probably couldn't play the trumpet very well.

Peter Drucker

❖ ❖ ❖

Concentration is the secret of strengths in politics, in war,
in trade, in short in all management of human affairs.

Ralph Waldo Emerson

❖ ❖ ❖

Most of what we say and do is not essential. If you can eliminate it,
you'll have more time, and more tranquility. Ask yourself at
every moment, "Is this necessary?"

Marcus Aurelius, *Meditations*

❖ ❖ ❖

If I had eight hours to chop down a tree, I'd spend six sharpening my axe.

Abraham Lincoln

❖ ❖ ❖

If I miss a day of practice, I know it. If I miss two days, my manager knows it.
If I miss three days, my audience knows it.

André Previn

❖ ❖ ❖

Do I Escape the Day to Day Whirlwind and Tyranny of the Urgent?

The whirlwind is all the work you do every day just to keep things going. It is all about the urgent priorities that come at you and demand your immediate attention. And there are usually immediate consequences if you ignore the whirlwind; just don't respond to e-mail or voice mail for a couple of days and see how interesting your life gets! An organization's top goals, on the other hand, have to do with what is ultimately most important and often lack the feel of urgency. You have to carve out time for the top goals or they don't happen. Urgency almost always trumps importance.

Larry Bossidy and Ram Charan, *Execution: The Discipline of Getting Things Done*

❖ ❖ ❖

The real execution challenge is not simply achieving a goal. Your organization is filled with accomplished people who know how to achieve a goal. The real execution challenge is executing a goal in the midst of the whirlwind!

Larry Bossidy and Ram Charan, *Execution: The Discipline of Getting Things Done*

❖ ❖ ❖

Sixty percent of managers are either distracted or disengaged from key organizational objectives. Many managers are confusing constant motion with constructive action, they are noted for their unproductive busy-ness.

Bruchand Ghoshal, HBS

❖ ❖ ❖

Our view of time either as an infinite or finite resource will directly affect the energy, time, and attention given to all relationships and activities.

Roger Merrill

❖ ❖ ❖

You have to decide what your highest priorities are and have the courage— pleasantly, smilingly, unapologetically—to say no to other things. And the way you do that is by having a bigger "yes" burning inside.

Stephen R. Covey

❖ ❖ ❖

Chaos is inherent in all compounded things. Strive on with diligence.

Buddha

❖ ❖ ❖

We have a limited number of resources. What is the best focus that we can have? All key decisions can be characterized by focus, focus, focus.

Meg Whitman

❖ ❖ ❖

Concentration comes out of a combination of confidence and hunger.

Arnold Palmer

❖ ❖ ❖

Within each individual lies the need for meaning—the longing to be of value. This craving for purpose propels us to make the choices that will bring us the mot joy and satisfaction from life. But in a busy world, it is so easy to become diverted by lesser choices—choices that in the long run are of little value or meaning. And so to gain the peace of mind and sense of accomplishment that we desire, we must pause momentarily to develop a clear image of the dreams, priorities, and goals that we believe will have the most lasting meaning, both for us and for others.

Stephen R. Covey, *Everyday Greatness*

❖ ❖ ❖

The vital task rarely must be done today or even this week. The urgent task calls for instant action. The momentary appeal of these tasks seems irresistible and they devour our energy. But in the light of time's perspective their deceptive promise fades. With a sense of loss, we recall the vital task we pushed aside. We realize we have become slaves to the tyranny of the urgent.

Charles E. Hummel

❖ ❖ ❖

I have found in running businesses that the best results come from letting high-grade people work unencumbered.

Warren Buffett

❖ ❖ ❖

Beware of the barrenness of a busy life.

Socrates

❖ ❖ ❖

They intoxicate themselves with work so they won't see how they really are.

Aldous Huxley

❖ ❖ ❖

Indecision is debilitating; it feeds upon itself it is, one might almost say, habit-forming. Not only that, but it is contagious; it transmits itself to others . . ..
Business is dependent upon action. It cannot go forward by hesitation.
Those in executive positions must fortify themselves with facts and accept responsibility for decisions based upon them. Often greater risk is involved in postponement than in making a wrong decision.

Harry A. Hopf, *Thoughts On Leadership*

❖ ❖ ❖

We all have two selves—an inner self that is thoughtful, reflective, and a good listener; and an outer task-oriented self. Our inner self is focused on connecting with people and finding significance in life; while our outer, task-oriented self is focused on achieving, and often too busy to learn.

To avoid the rat race and stay on course, we must honor our inner selves. The only way to do that is to seek out times of solitude when we can be alone with the voice that says, "You are a loved and valuable person."   Solitude is hard to find.
Therefore, I recommend that people enter their day slowly by engaging in an activity that is intrinsically valuable and noncompetitive such as prayer, meditation, reflective reading, or certain kinds of exercise. Walking, running swimming, biking, and other activities that allow you to reflect while you are doing them perfect.

Ken Blanchard, *The Heart of a Leader*

❖ ❖ ❖

Most of the significant advances in human history—great social and political reformations, artistic productions, unique inventions, etc.—have come not from rushing around but from being still. They require periods of deep and rigorous contemplation, for only in this way can we escape the clamor of outer voices that remind us of "how we've always done it."

How do we find this time for solitude and introspection? We must stake it out for ourselves. One top manager I know does not allow his people to talk on the phone or meet between 8:30 and 9:30 in the morning. This is their quiet time. I used to talk to people on airplanes. Now I use that time to reflect, read, write, or just quiet my mind. I am amazed by my creativity after a long flight.

Ken Blanchard, *The Heart of a Leader*

❖ ❖ ❖

Do I Show Empathy and Understanding?

It is everyone's best interest to understand one another and to find as much common ground as possible.

President Jimmy Carter

❖ ❖ ❖

We have two ears and one mouth so that we can listen twice as much as we speak.

Epictetus

❖ ❖ ❖

In a controversy the instant we feel anger we have already ceased striving for the truth, and have begun striving for ourselves.

Buddha

❖ ❖ ❖

If there is any one secret of success, it lies in the ability to get the other person's point of view and see things from his angle as well as your own.

Henry Ford, *Everyday Greatness,* by Stephen R. Covey

❖ ❖ ❖

Acknowledging other people is a powerful sign that you recognize that they are important and worthwhile. A person is a person only because of other people.

Zulu Folk Saying

❖ ❖ ❖

Men love with their eyes. Women love with their ears.

Zsa Zsa Gabor

❖ ❖ ❖

Empathic listening involves more than words. The total impact of a message is 7% verbal, 38% vocal including tone and inflection, and 55% is non-verbal queues.

Albert Mehrabian

❖ ❖ ❖

Let us not look back in anger or forward in fear, but around in awareness.

James Thurber

❖ ❖ ❖

Who is the person who is wise? The one who has the ability to learn something from every person. A wise person is one who is able to really hear and appreciate every individual.

Rabbi Jeffrey Summit

❖ ❖ ❖

The verbal component of a face-to-face conversation is less than 35% and over 65% of communication is done nonverbally.

Ray Birdwhistell

❖ ❖ ❖

Remember that I'm human. Before you judge me or decide how you'll deal with me, walk in my shoes. If you do, I think you'll find with more understanding we can meet in the middle and walk the rest of the ay together.

Eric Harvey and Steve Ventura

❖ ❖ ❖

They (Montreal Canadian Expos fans) discovered "boo" is pronounced the same in French as it is in English.

Harry Caray

❖ ❖ ❖

Leaders, beware! The higher you go in an organization, the less likely people are to give you straight feedback. Feedback is your life-support system. Without it, you will eventually fail. Do everything you can to create a culture where it is safe to give you feedback.

Stephen R. Covey

❖ ❖ ❖

No one wants advice—only corroboration.

John Steinbeck

❖ ❖ ❖

No one really listens to anyone else, and if you try it for a while you'll see why.

Mignon McLaughlin

❖ ❖ ❖

Talk to people about themselves and they will listen for hours.

Benjamin Disraeli

❖ ❖ ❖

There is no such thing as conversation. It is an illusion.
There are intersecting monologues, that is all.

Rebecca West

❖ ❖ ❖

The one way to prevent conversation from being boring is to say the wrong thing.

Frank Sheed

❖ ❖ ❖

Advice is what we ask for when we already know the answer but wish we didn't.

Erica Jong

❖ ❖ ❖

The only thing to do with good advice is to pass it along. It is never of use to
oneself.

Oscar Wilde

❖ ❖ ❖

In Zen they say: If it is boring after two minutes listen to it four. If it is still boring,
listen for eight or sixteen or thirty-two minutes, and so on. Soon we discover that
it is not boring at all but actually very interesting.

John Cage

❖ ❖ ❖

Never look back unless you are planning to go that way.

Henry David Thoreau

❖ ❖ ❖

Don't confuse me with facts. My mind is already made up.

Author Unknown

❖ ❖ ❖

Know thyself, the unexamined life is not worth living.

Socrates

❖ ❖ ❖

Let the wise listen and learn yet more.

Proverbs 1:5

❖ ❖ ❖

He who holds his tongue is wise.

Proverbs 10:19

❖ ❖ ❖

People only see what they are prepared to see.

Ralph Waldo Emerson

❖ ❖ ❖

The examined life is no picnic.

Robert Folgham

❖ ❖ ❖

We cannot all know. All we can do is try to listen carefully and with full attention to each voice as it addresses the divine.

Huston Smith

❖ ❖ ❖

Think about the feedback as "a gift" from your boss, peers, and direct reports.

Lex Watterson

❖ ❖ ❖

What we think, believe, and say is, in the end, of little consequence.
The only thing that is of real consequence is what we do.

John Ruskin

❖ ❖ ❖

If I had 1 hour to solve a problem, I would spend 55 minutes understanding the problem and 5 minutes solving the problem.

Albert Einstein

❖ ❖ ❖

The greatest need of the human soul is to be understood.

Stephen R. Covey

❖ ❖ ❖

Unexpressed feelings never die but are buried alive and manifest themselves in ugly ways.

Stephen R. Covey

❖ ❖ ❖

I like talking to a brick wall, it's the only thing in the world that never contradicts me.

Oscar Wilde

❖ ❖ ❖

Never miss a good chance to shut up and listen.

Will Rogers

❖ ❖ ❖

Scarecrow: I haven't got a brain...only straw. Dorothy: How can you talk if you haven't got a brain? Scarecrow: I don't know...but some people without brains do an awful lot of talking, don't they? Dorothy: Yes, I guess you're right.

The Wizard of Oz

❖ ❖ ❖

Respect for the right of another to be right or wrong does not mean that the wrong is right.

Ravi Zacharias

❖ ❖ ❖

Everything that irritates us about others can lead us to an understanding of ourselves.

Carl Jung

❖ ❖ ❖

Judgment prevents us from seeing the good that lies beyond appearances.

Wayne Dyer

❖ ❖ ❖

The capacity for delight is the gift of paying attention.

Julia Margaret Cameron

❖ ❖ ❖

Life is denied by lack of attention, whether it be to cleaning
a window or writing a masterpiece.

Nadia Boulanger

❖ ❖ ❖

The moment one gives close attention to anything, even a blade of grass, it
becomes a mysterious, awesome, indescribably magnificent world in itself.

Jose Ortega Y Gasset

❖ ❖ ❖

It's a rare person who wants to hear what he doesn't want to hear.

Dick Cavett

❖ ❖ ❖

People who are able to help others soothe their feelings have an especially
valued social commodity; they are the souls others turn to when in the
greatest emotional need. We are all part of each other's tool kit for
emotional change, for better or for worse.

Daniel Goleman, *Emotional Intelligence*

❖ ❖ ❖

There is no one who does not sometime need to be forgiven, and there is no one
who does not hope that his errors will be forgotten. But a verbally proffered
forgiveness comes much easier than an actually accomplished forgetfulness. And
if every time we are miffed, we remind a man of all his past mistakes, we haven't
fully forgiven.

Richard L. Evans, *Vital Quotations*

❖ ❖ ❖

But let judgment run down as waters, and righteousness as a mighty stream.

Amos 5:24

❖ ❖ ❖

Kind words can be short and easy to speak, but their echoes are truly endless.

Mother Teresa, *Everyday Greatness,* by Stephen R. Covey

❖ ❖ ❖

The ability to control your emotions and actions in response to indignities done by others is becoming increasingly rare in today's litigious society. Yet such control is at the very core of the principle of magnanimity. For a magnanimous person is one who rejects revenge and rises above anger while in pursuit of more worthy ends.

One who knew well the meaning of magnanimity was Mahatma Gandhi. Throughout his life there were many occasions when he could easily have allowed anger to govern his thoughts and actions. But instead, he chose magnanimity over revenge as his guide for making decisions. In the process, he greatly influenced those near to him.

Stephen R. Covey, *Everyday Greatness*

❖ ❖ ❖

A gentle word, a kind look, a good-natured smile can work wonders and accomplish miracles. There is a secret pride in every human heart that revolts at tyranny. You may order and drive an individual, but you cannot make him respect you.

William Hazlitt, *Thoughts On Leadership*

❖ ❖ ❖

A quick and sound judgment, good common sense, kind feeling, and an instinctive perception of character, in these are the elements of what is called tact, which has so much to do with acceptability and success in life.

Charles Simmons, *Thoughts On Success*

❖ ❖ ❖

One of the leading reasons for a lack of magnanimity is what I call a scarcity mentality. People with a scarcity mentality think there is only so much in the world to go around. It's as if they see life as a pie. When another person gets a big piece, then they get less. Such people are always trying to get even, trying to pull others down to their level so they can get an equal or even bigger piece of the pie. But it is an abundance mentality and a feeling of inner security that truly are at the root of magnanimity. And though magnanimity may not be an everyday term, it will always be one of the most distinguishing characteristics of Everyday Greatness.

Stephen R. Covey, *Everyday Greatness*

❖ ❖ ❖

We are all aware that there are many mountains in need of moving. Mountains of ignorance and intolerance need to be transformed into peaks of understanding and acceptance, mountains of materialism must be lowered, and mountains of inequality must be transformed into partnership, respect, and egalitarianism.

Sue Patton Thoele, *Woman's Book of Sou*

❖ ❖ ❖

Strengthen your heart. If you're not as caring toward others as you could be, you need to get the focus off yourself. Make a list of little things you could do to add value to friends and colleagues. Then try to do one of them every day. Don't wait until you feel like it to help others. Act your way into feeling.

John C. Maxwell, *The 21 Indispensable Qualities of a Leader*

❖ ❖ ❖

Do I Act with Integrity?

The bedrock of character is self-discipline; the virtuous life, as philosophers since Aristotle have observed, is based on self-control. A related keystone of character is being able to motivate and guide oneself, whether in doing homework, finish a job, or getting up in the morning. Add, as we have seen, the ability to defer gratification and to control and channel one's urges to act is a basic emotional skill, one that in a former day was called will. "We need to be in control of ourselves—our appetites, our passions—to do right by others," notes Thomas Lickona, writing about character education. "It takes will to keep emotion under the control of reason."

Daniel Goleman, *Emotional Intelligence*

❖ ❖ ❖

Although I am a convinced democrat I know well that the human community would stagnate and even degenerate without a minority of socially conscious and upright men and women willing to make sacrifices for their convictions.

Albert Einstein, *Bite-Size Einstein*

❖ ❖ ❖

Colin Powell is regarded as a man of great integrity. In a recent interview, he pointed on his desk to one of his most prized possessions, a photo of Ronald Reagan and Powell. The photo was inscribed by Reagan as follows: "Colin, when you tell me something I know it is so."   As a leader, you could receive no greater compliment.

Mac Anderson, *The Essence of Leadership*

❖ ❖ ❖

We might say that humility is the mother of all virtues, including integrity, and that courage is the father. When people follow true principles courageously in difficult and tempting circumstances, they cultivate integrity and personal security. Their sense of worth does not come from being compared with others, and therefore, they develop an abundance mentality—seeing life as a cornucopia of resources and opportunities.

Stephen R. Covey, forward, *Business with Integrity*

❖ ❖ ❖

Integrity usually extracts a price. To be a person of integrity
we must be willing to pay that price.

Ned C. Hill, *Business with Integrity*

❖ ❖ ❖

The integrity of a person is the measure of how consistent that person is from the inside to the outside. A person of high integrity is who he or she claims to be. Such a person of integrity performs under the pressure of real and demanding situations—not just when it is easy. It's one thing to be a ladder standing in my garage; but the real test of that ladder is when it has to perform under pressure. Likewise it is relatively easy to claim to stand for certain values when the pressure is off—but much more difficult to live those values when life's pressures come.

Ned C. Hill, *Business with Integrity*

❖ ❖ ❖

A senior executive from one of our advertising agencies got into a cab in New York and found a computer disk lying on the floorboard that included the marketing plans from one of our toughest competitors. If that had happened to you, what would you have done with the disk? What would you have expected someone who worked for you, an employee or a supplier, to do with that disk? I am pleased to say that in this case the agency executive sent the disk back to the chairman of the competitive company, assuring him that neither the agency nor anyone at Procter had looked at the contents of the disk. As his letter said, "We always compete with commitment and intensity, but we'll never compromise our ethics to win."

John E. Pepper, *Business with Integrity*

❖ ❖ ❖

There is no such thing as a minor lapse of integrity.

Tom Peters, *If Ignorance Is Bliss, Why Aren't There More Happy People?*

❖ ❖ ❖

The person who stands out in the crowd demonstrates that he has his own set of values and has a strong sense of self-worth. While the winds of conflicting ideas blow some people away, and the tides of various fads wash others away, he will stand firm.

David J. Mahoney, *Confessions of a Street-smart Manager*

❖ ❖ ❖

Nearly all men can stand adversity, but if you want to test a man's character, give him power.

Abraham Lincoln, Thoughts on Leadership

❖ ❖ ❖

The spirit of an organization is created from the top. The proof of sincerity and seriousness of a management is uncompromising emphasis on integrity of character. This, above all, has to be symbolized in management's "people" decisions. For it is character through which leadership is exercised; it is character that sets the example and is imitated. Character is not something one can fool people about. The people with whom a person works, and especially subordinates, know in a few weeks whether he or she has integrity or not. They may forgive a person for a great deal: incompetence, ignorance, insecurity, or bad manners. But they will not forgive a lack of integrity in that person. Nor will they forgive higher management for choosing him. This is particularly true of the people at the head of an enterprise. For the spirit of an organization is created from the top. If an organization is great in spirit, it is because the spirit of its top people is great. If it decays, it does so because the top rots; as the proverb has it, "Trees die from the top." No one should ever be appointed to a senior position unless top management is willing to have his or her character serve as the model for subordinates.

Peter F. Drucker, "Management: Tasks, Responsibilities, Practices", *The Daily Drucker*

❖ ❖ ❖

I have never been able to conceive how any rational being could propose happiness to himself from the exercise of power over others.

Thomas Jefferson, *Thoughts On Leadership*

❖ ❖ ❖

The first quality of a relational leader is the ability to understand how people feel and think. As you work with others, recognize that all people, whether leaders or followers, have some things in common:

They like to feel special, so sincerely compliment them.

They want a better tomorrow, so show them hope.

They desire direction, so navigate for them.

They are selfish, so speak to their needs first.

They get low emotionally, so encourage them.

They want success, so help them win.

Recognizing these truths, a leader must still be able to treat people as individuals. The ability to look at each person, understand him, and connect with him is a major factor in relational success.

John C. Maxwell, The 21 Indispensable Qualities of a Leader

❖ ❖ ❖

There is a time when integrity should take the rudder from team loyalty.

Thomas J. Watson, Jr., *Fortune,* 1977, *The Manager's Book of Quotations*

❖ ❖ ❖

The greater a man is in power above others, the more he ought to excel them in virtue. None ought to govern who is not better than the governed.

Publius Syrus

❖ ❖ ❖

Leadership is a potent combination of strategy and character. But if you must be without one, be without the strategy.

Norman Schwarzkopf

❖ ❖ ❖

Integrity is telling myself the Truth. Honesty is telling the Truth to other people.

Spencer Johnson

❖ ❖ ❖

This above all: to thine own self be true, And it must follow, as the night the day, Thou canst not then be false to any man.

William Shakespeare

❖ ❖ ❖

The time is always right to do what is right.

Martin Luther King, Jr.

❖ ❖ ❖

Try not to become a man of success but rather try to become a man of value.

Albert Einstein

❖ ❖ ❖

And as we let our own light shine, we unconsciously give other people permission to do the same.

Marianne Williamson

❖ ❖ ❖

Nobody can acquire honor by doing what is wrong.

Thomas Jefferson

❖ ❖ ❖

The glue that holds all relationships together—including the relationship between the leader and the led—is trust; and trust is based on integrity.

Brian Tracy

❖ ❖ ❖

Establish core values, principles, and beliefs. In today's rapidly changing global marketplace, it is critical for organizations to effectively navigate in a permanent whitewater world... To do this, leaders need a changeless foundation of values and principles. This changeless core gives people the capacity to deal with the dynamic changes and forces that surround them.

Stephen R. Covey

❖ ❖ ❖

How Do I Lead My Team?

Everyone pays lip service to the idea that leading an organization requires strength of character. In execution it's absolutely critical. Without what we call emotional fortitude, you can't be honest with yourself, deal honestly with business and organizational realities, or give people forthright assessments. You can't tolerate the diversity of viewpoints, mental architectures, and personal backgrounds that organizations need in their members in order to avoid becoming ingrown. If you can't do these things, you can't execute.

Larry Bossidy and Ram Charan, *Execution: The Discipline of Getting Things Done*

❖ ❖ ❖

Candid dialogue is live ammunition of execution.

Larry Bossidy and Ram Charan

❖ ❖ ❖

Complete transparency in performance evaluations need to be candid and frequent. It is foundational for management assesses both values and performance. Performance is a ticket to the game, and adherence to values is what gets you promoted.

Jack Welch

❖ ❖ ❖

Good leaders are committed to helping their people win. When someone fails, they accept responsibility for that failure. I think anytime you fire someone who works for you or anytime you're looking for a place to hide someone who works for you (Lawrence Peter called this "a lateral arabesque"), step up to a mirror and take a peek. In most cases, the biggest cause of the problem is looking you in the eyes.
The main job of a leader is to help his or her people succeed in accomplishing their goals. And when people accomplish their goals and win, everyone wins.

Ken Blanchard, *The Heart of a Leader*

❖ ❖ ❖

The only certain measure of success is to render more and better service than is expected of you.

Og Mandino, *Chicken Soup for the Soul at Work*

❖ ❖ ❖

No one can live on a level inconsistent with the way he sees himself. You may have observed that in people. If someone sees himself as a loser, he finds a way to lose. Anytime his success surpasses his security, the result is self-destruction. That's not only true for followers, but it's also true for leaders.

Insecure leaders are dangerous—to themselves, their follower, and the organizations they lead---because a leadership position amplifies personal flaws. Whatever negative baggage you have in life only gets more difficult to bear when you're trying to lead others.

John C. Maxwell, *The 21 Indispensable Qualities of a Leader*

❖ ❖ ❖

Vision is everything for a leader. It is utterly indispensable. Why? Because vision leads the leader. It paints the target. It sparks and fuels the fire within, and draws him forward. It is also the fire lighter for others who follow that leader. Show me a leader without vision, and I'll show you someone who isn't going anywhere. At best he is traveling in circles.
To get a handle on vision and how it comes to be a part of good leader's life, understand these things:

Vision Starts Within

Vision Draws on Your History

Vision Meets Others' Needs

Vision Helps You Gather Resources

John C. Maxwell, *The 21 Indispensable Qualities of a Leader*

❖ ❖ ❖

When the conduct of men is designed to be influenced, persuasion, kind, unassuming persuasion, should ever be adopted. It is an old and a true maxim, that a "drop of honey catches more flies than a gallon of gall."

Abraham Lincoln, *Temperance Address, February 22, 1842*

❖ ❖ ❖

To lead people, walk beside them ... As for the best leaders, the people do not notice their existence. The next best, the people honor and praise. The next, the people fear; and the next, the people hate ... When the best leader's work is done the people say, 'We did it ourselves!'

Lao Tzu

❖ ❖ ❖

Do I Lead with Persistence?

Persistence means sticking to your guns. It's keeping your commitment and making your actions consistent with your word. It's all about "walking your talk."

Ken Blanchard, *The Heart of a Leader*

❖ ❖ ❖

Vacillating people seldom succeed. They seldom win the solid respect of their fellows. Successful men and women are very careful in reaching decisions and very persistent and determined in action thereafter.

L.G. Elliott, *Thoughts On Success*

❖ ❖ ❖

Ray Kroc, at 51, tried for two years and talks to more than one hundred people trying to raise the money to start McDonald's. Walt Disney failed miserably in his first four attempts to live his dream. Henry Ford went bankrupt seven times while trying to launch Ford Motor Company.

Mac Anderson, *The Essence of Leadership*

❖ ❖ ❖

The slogan "press on" has solved and always will solve the problems of the human race.

Calvin Coolidge, *Business with Integrity*

❖ ❖ ❖

I found that the men and women who got to the top were those who did the jobs they had in hand, with everything they had of energy, enthusiasm and hard work.

Harry S. Truman, *Thoughts On Leadership*

❖ ❖ ❖

There is a fine line between persistence and obstinacy. I have come to realize the key is to choose a problem that is worth persistent effort.

Dr. Judah Folkman, *Yes I Can,* by Fran Lostys

❖ ❖ ❖

A bold onset is half the battle.

Giuseppe Garibaldi

❖ ❖ ❖

Constant dripping hollows out a stone.

Lucretius

❖ ❖ ❖

If the people knew how hard I had to work to gain my mastery,
it wouldn't seem wonderful at all.

Michelangelo

❖ ❖ ❖

Nothing in this world can take the place of persistence. Talent will not; nothing is more common than unsuccessful men with talent. Genius will not; unrewarded genius is almost a proverb. Education will not; the world is full of educated derelicts. Persistence and determination alone are omnipotent.

Calvin Coolidge

❖ ❖ ❖

Do I Make Sure My Team Contributes to the Organization's Mission?

A committee is a group of the unwilling, chosen from the unfit to do the unnecessary.

Author Unknown

❖ ❖ ❖

One question has to be asked to decide "What should I contribute?" *"Where and how can I have results that make a difference?"* The answer to this question has to balance a number of things. Results should be hard to achieve. They should require "stretching," to use the present buzzword. But they should be within reach. To aim at results that cannot be achieved—or can be achieved only under the most unlikely circumstances—is not being "ambitious." It is being foolish. At the same time, results should be meaningful. They should make a difference. And they should be visible and, if at all possible, measurable.

The decision about "What should my contribution be?" balances three elements. First comes the question: "What does the situation require?" then comes the question: "How could I make the greatest contribution, with my strengths, my way of performing, my values, to what needs to be done?" Finally, there is the question: "What results have to be achieved to make a difference?" This then leads to the *action conclusions:* what to do, where to start, how to start, what goals and deadlines to set.

Peter F. Drucker, "Management Challenges for the 21st Century", *The Daily Drucker*

❖ ❖ ❖

Management is the art of getting three men to do three men's work.

William Feather, Thoughts on Leadership

❖ ❖ ❖

Do I Grasp the Basic Principles of Leading a Team?

A leader takes people where they want to go. A great leader takes people where they don't necessarily want to go, but ought to be.

Rosalynn Carter

❖ ❖ ❖

Team performance almost always depends on how well team leaders . . . strike a critical balance between doing things themselves and letting other people do them.   In this, too, attitude is key. Team leaders genuinely believe that they do *not* have all the answers—so they do not insist on providing them. They believe they do *not* need to make all key decisions—so they do not do so. They believe they *cannot* succeed without the combined contributions of all the other members of the team to a common end—and so they avoid any action that might constrain inputs or intimidate anyone on the team. Ego is *not* their predominant concern. Such behaviors are neither difficult to learn or practice. . . . But few of us practice such things automatically, especially in business contexts where authority typically means the ability to command and control subordinates and to make all the tough decisions.

Jon R. Katzenbach and Douglas K. Smith, "The Wisdom of Teams", *Harper Business*, 1993

❖ ❖ ❖

Power can be seen as power with rather than power over, and it can be used for competence and cooperation, rather than dominance and control.

Anne L. Barstow

❖ ❖ ❖

When they discover the centre of the universe, a lot of people will be disappointed to discover they are not it.

Bernard Bailey

❖ ❖ ❖

A boss creates fear, a leader confidence. A boss fixes blame, a leader corrects mistakes. A boss knows all, a leader asks questions. A boss makes work drudgery, a leader makes it interesting. A boss is interested in himself or herself, a leader is interested in the group.

Russell H. Ewing, *If Ignorance Is Bliss, Why Aren't There More Happy People?*

❖ ❖ ❖

Do I Establish Clear Goals, Achievable and Wildly Important?

High expectations are the key to everything.

Sam Walton, *Leadership Through the Ages*, by Rudolph W. Giuliani

❖ ❖ ❖

A team's mission should be clear. Written or unwritten, it should be directly linked to and supportive of the organization's mission. Having a mission is good, but it is not enough. For the mission to be effective, there must be consensus among team members and stakeholders about the mission itself and how it relates to the organization's mission and strategic direction. . . . Specific short-term and
long-term goals establish an understanding of the resources, skills, time and support that the team will need to succeed.

Paula Chronister and Tig Williams, *Creating Better Teams: Five Dimensions of Designing, Implementing, and Sustaining Effective Teams,*1996

❖ ❖ ❖

The hunger for performance is far more important to team success than team-building exercises, special incentives, or team leaders with ideal profiles.

Jon R. Katzenbach and Douglas K. Smith, "The Wisdom of Teams",
Harper Business, 1993

❖ ❖ ❖

Focus is what helps us overcome whatever is distracting us.

Timothy Gallwey

❖ ❖ ❖

I long to accomplish a great and noble task; but it is my chief duty to accomplish small tasks as if they were great and noble.

Helen Keller

❖ ❖ ❖

Leaders known for getting results focus totally on a limited agenda of clear core objectives and they keep their people constantly and measurably moving forward on those objectives.

John Kotter

❖ ❖ ❖

Wanting to be better in performance is like wanting to be happy—it is very difficult to get there directly. It is much wiser first, to focus on the building blocks.
And, in the case of performance, the building blocks are commitment, resilience, and ruthless disregard for distractions.

Laura Teresa Marquez

❖ ❖ ❖

The most creative and productive work comes when people freely make commitments to one another, not when bosses tell them what to do.

Jim Collins, *Good to Great*

❖ ❖ ❖

High expectations are the key to everything.

Sam Walton, *Leadership Through the Ages*, by Rudolph W. Giuliani

❖ ❖ ❖

Goals cannot sound noble but vague. Targets cannot be so blurry they can't be hit. Your direction has to be so vivid that if you randomly woke one of your employees in the middle of the night and asked him, 'Where are we going?' he could still answer in a half-asleep stupor.

Jack Welch

❖ ❖ ❖

I always wanted to be somebody, but I should have been more specific.

Lily Tomlin

❖ ❖ ❖

I believe in God, only I spell it nature.

Frank Lloyd Wright

❖ ❖ ❖

When you make a mistake, don't look back at it long. Take the reason of the thing into your mind and then look forward. Mistakes are lessons of wisdom. The past cannot be changed. The future is yet in your power.

Hugh White

❖ ❖ ❖

The difference between what we are doing and what we're capable of doing would solve most of the world's problems.

Gandhi

❖ ❖ ❖

My personal philosophy is not to undertake a project unless it is manifestly important and nearly impossible.

Edwin Land, *If Ignorance Is Bliss, Why Aren't There More Happy People?*

❖ ❖ ❖

Ninety percent of managers are typically either distracted or disengaged from key organizational objectives, "confusing frenetic motion with constructive action."

H Bruch and S Ghosal, *Beware the Busy Manager*

❖ ❖ ❖

A successful life does not result from chance; nor is it determined by fate or good fortune, but rather through a succession of successful days.

Ari Kiev, *A Strategy for Daily Living*

❖ ❖ ❖

No one ever accomplishes anything of consequence without a goal . . . Goal setting is the strongest human force for self-motivation.

Paul Myer

❖ ❖ ❖

In absence of clearly defined goals, we become strangely loyal to performing daily acts of trivia.

Author Unknown

❖ ❖ ❖

Nothing can add more power to your life than concentrating all your energies on a limited set of targets.

Nido Qubein

❖ ❖ ❖

The goal defines the team not the organizational structure.

Jim Stuart

❖ ❖ ❖

"Which player am I?" What game am I playing? I was winning, but I didn't understand the game. I didn't even know what player I was. This was much less satisfying than other games where I understood the rules—even when I lost horribly.

People want to be challenged. This doesn't mean you should set goals that no one can reach, but don't be afraid of setting and communicating your goals to the people you lead. This is your job as a leader—to show people where you are going and how you are going to measure your progress. If you don't give people these goals, it is hard for them to really get satisfaction from their job.

Mark Shead

❖ ❖ ❖

The Critical Wildly Important Goals (WIG) Question: Within the next year or less, what 1 or 2 WIGs or Projects must we achieve with excellence—or nothing else we achieve will really matter?

Great teams are totally clear on the "Wildly Important Goals." While any important goal is worth achieving, a Wildly Important Goal *must* be achieved. Failure to do so renders any of your other achievements inconsequential.

Execution Essentials

❖ ❖ ❖

All companies have goals. But there is a difference between merely having a goal and becoming committed to a huge, daunting challenge—like a big mountain to climb. Such a goal—a big, hairy, audacious goal—is clear and compelling and serves as a unifying focal point of effort.

Jim Collins

❖ ❖ ❖

Effective leaders check their performance. They write down, "What do I hope to achieve if I take on this assignment?" . . . and then come back and check their performance against goals. This way, they find out whether they picked the truly important things to do. I've seen a great many people who are exceedingly good at execution, but exceedingly poor at picking the important things. They are magnificent at getting the unimportant things done. They have an impressive record of achievement on trivial matters."

Peter Drucker

❖ ❖ ❖

The reason most people never reach their goals is that they don't define them . . .
Winners can tell you where they are going, what they plan to do along
the way, and who will be sharing the adventure with them.

Dennis Waitley

❖ ❖ ❖

The evidence is overwhelming that you cannot begin to achieve your best unless
you set some aim in life. What would football be without a goal? You see men
play over their heads to reach the goal, whether in sports or throughout life."

Henry J. Kaiser

❖ ❖ ❖

Without clear measures, the same goal will mean a hundred different things to a
hundred different people.

Jim Stuart

❖ ❖ ❖

There is always an abundance of good things that managers can go after.
You have to narrow the focus on your goals and priorities—leader's
eyes are always bigger than their stomachs.

Chris McChesney

❖ ❖ ❖

Character is formed, not by laws, commands, and decrees, but by
quiet influence, unconscious suggestion and personal guidance.

Marion L. Burton, *Thoughts on Leadership*

❖ ❖ ❖

You've got to think about "big things" while you're doing small things,
so that all the small things go in the right direction

Alvin Toffler, *Newsweek,* April 4, 1988, *The Manager's Book Of Quotations*

❖ ❖ ❖

Put something countable, something quantifiable in your goal so that you'll *know*
when you've obtained it. You are not stuck with this goal forever and ever. When
you reach it, you can choose a bigger one. For now, however, it's important to
know *what* your goal is, and be able to tell *when* you've reached it.

The Portable DO IT!

❖ ❖ ❖

An important way to motivate your people is to make sure they know where they are going. See that each person's goals are clearly defined and he or she knows what good performance looks like. This will give them a clear focus for their energy and put them on the road to becoming high performing, empowered producers.

Ken Blanchard, *The Heart of a Leader*

❖ ❖ ❖

All companies have goals. But there is a difference between merely having a goal and becoming committed to a huge, daunting challenge—like a big mountain to climb. Such a goal—a big, hairy audacious goal—is clear and compolling and serves as a unifying focal point of effort.

Jim Collins, *Management Essentials*

❖ ❖ ❖

To say what one means by a goal is to reduce neither the importance of the goal nor its profundity. Though the meaning, when seen on the paper, may appear trivial—or even *be* trivial—the act of writing it down means merely that what was
once secret is now open for inspection and improvement.

Robert F. Mager, *Executive Essentials*

❖ ❖ ❖

Hope, modern researchers are finding, does more than offer a bit of solace amid affliction; it plays a surprisingly potent role in life, offering an advantage in realms as diverse as school achievement and bearing up in onerous jobs. Hope, in a technical sense, is more than the sunny view that everything will turn out all right.
Snyder defines it with more specificity as "believing you have both the will and the way to accomplish your goals, whatever they may be.

Daniel Goleman, *Emotional Intelligence*

❖ ❖ ❖

Nothing great was ever achieved without enthusiasm.

Ralph Waldo Emerson, "Heroism", *The Manager's Book of Quotations*

❖ ❖ ❖

Obstacles are those frightful things you see when you take your eyes off the goal.

Hannah Moore, *Thoughts on Leadership*

❖ ❖ ❖

Robert J. Kriegel learned the value of taking life in little steps as a ski instructor, when taking novices to the edge of a difficult slope: "They would look all the way down to the bottom. Invariably the hill would seem too steep and too difficult, so they'd back away. I would tell them not to think of skiing the whole hill. Instead, just try making the first turn. This changed their focus. After a few turns they would become more confident and, without any prodding, take off down the slope."

Robert J. Kriegel with Louis Patler, *If It Ain't Broke, Break it*

❖ ❖ ❖

Every ceiling, when reached, becomes a floor, upon which one walks as a matter of course and prescriptive right.

Aldous Huxley

❖ ❖ ❖

It is not enough to take steps which may some day lead to a goal; each step must be itself a goal and a step likewise.

Johann Wolfgang von Goethe

❖ ❖ ❖

Do I Understand the Difference Between Goals and Values?

Sheldon Bowles and I, in our book *Gung Ho!*, make an important distinction between values and goals. The minute you proclaim a goal, it's real, it's set. Values don't work that way. Values become real only when you demonstrate them in the way you act and the way you insist others behave. Goals are for the future; values are for now. Goals are set; values are lived. Goals change; values are rocks you can count on . . .. When you know what you stand for, you can turn around on a dime and have five cents change.

Ken Blanchard, *The Heart of a Leader*

❖ ❖ ❖

Do I Establish a Team Infrastructure Proper to the Mission?

Teams need an underlying structure to support them. This structure is determined by the size and composition of teams, as well as the management systems that identify supporting policies and procedures, and the alignment of personal performance measures, rewards, and compensation.

aula Chronister and Tig Williams, *Creating Better Teams: Five Dimensions of Designing, Implementing, and Sustaining Effective Teams*

❖ ❖ ❖

When the infrastructure shifts, everything rumbles.

Stan Davis

❖ ❖ ❖

People may be said to resemble not the bricks of which a house is built, but the pieces of a picture puzzle, each differing in shape, but matching the rest, and thus bringing out the picture.

Felix Adler

❖ ❖ ❖

Do I Teach as Well as Learn?

The whole art of teaching is only the art of awakening the natural curiosity of young minds for the purpose of satisfying it afterwards; and curiosity itself can be vivid and wholesome only in proportion as the mind is contented and happy.

Anatole France

❖ ❖ ❖

Education is the leading of human souls to what is best, and making what is best out of them; and these two objects are always attainable together, and by the same means. The training which makes men happiest in themselves also makes them most serviceable to others.

John Ruski

❖ ❖ ❖

There is only one thing that will really train the human mind and that is the voluntary use of the mind by the man himself. You may aid him, you may guide him, you may suggest to him, and, above all else, you may inspire him. But the only thing worth having is that which he gets by his own exertions, and what he gets is in direct proportion to what he puts into it.

Albert L. Lowell

❖ ❖ ❖

The moment a leader allows himself to become the primary reality people worry about, rather than reality being the primary reality, you have a recipe for mediocrity, or worse. This is one of the key reasons why less charismatic leaders often produce better long-term results than their more charismatic counterparts.

Indeed, for those of you with a strong, charismatic personality, it is worthwhile to consider the idea that charisma can be as much a liability as an asset. Your strength of personality can sow the seeds of problems, when people filter the brutal facts from you. You can overcome the liabilities of having charisma, but it does require conscious attention.

Jim Collins, *Good to Great*

❖ ❖ ❖

The mind is like a parachute. It doesn't work if it's not open.

Frank Zappa, *If Ignorance Is Bliss, Why Aren't There More Happy People?*

❖ ❖ ❖

Leaders face the danger of contentment with the *status quo.* After all, if a leader already possesses influence and has achieved a level of respect, why should he keep growing? The answer is simple:

Your growth determines who you are.

Who you are determines who you attract.

Who you attract determines the success of your organization.

If you want to grow your organization, *you* have to remain teachable.

Allow me to give you five guidelines to help you cultivate and maintain a teachable attitude:

Cure Your Destination Disease

Overcome Your Success

3.Swear Off Shortcuts

Trade In Your Pride

Never Pay Twice for the Same Mistake

John C. Maxwell, *The 21 Indispensable Qualities of a Leader*

❖ ❖ ❖

The illiterate of the 21st century will not be those who cannot read and write but those who cannot learn, unlearn, and relearn.

Alvin Toffler

❖ ❖ ❖

If you can't explain it simply, you don't understand it well.

Albert Einstein

❖ ❖ ❖

Simplicity is the ultimate form of sophistication.

Leonardo Da Vinci

❖ ❖ ❖

Do I Plan Thoroughly?

Everybody has a game plan until somebody gets punched in the mouth.

Mike Tyson

❖ ❖ ❖

Everybody has a battle strategy until someone fires the first shot.

General David S. Patton

❖ ❖ ❖

I don't go to where the hockey puck is, I go to where I think it will be.

Wayne Gretzky

❖ ❖ ❖

Details often kill initiative, but there have been few successful men who weren't good at details. Don't ignore details. Lick them.

William B. Given, Jr., *Thoughts On Success*

❖ ❖ ❖

Every moment spent planning saves three or four in execution.

Crawford Greenwalt, Mackenzie, "The Time Trap", *The Manager's Book of Quotations*

❖ ❖ ❖

Unpredictability cannot be removed, or perhaps even substantially reduced, by excessive planning.

Tom Peters, "Thriving on Chaos", *The Manager's Book of Quotations*

❖ ❖ ❖

Consider the little mouse, how sagacious an animal it is which never entrusts its life to one hole only.

Plautus, "Truculentus", *The Manager's Book of Quotations*

❖ ❖ ❖

Don't cross a bridge until you come to it, and then be sure there's a bridge.

Anonymous, *The Manager's Book of Quotations*

❖ ❖ ❖

I was a great admirer of old D.H. Burnham of Chicago, who organized the Chicago regional planning, and he had a motto over his mantel on which was written, "MAKE NO LITTLE PLANS." You can always amend a big plan, but you can never expand a little one. I don't believe in little plans. I believe in plans big enough to meet a situation which we can't possible foresee now.

Harry S. Truman, Speech, November 2, 1949, *The Manager's Book of Quotations*

❖ ❖ ❖

Everything is both simpler than we can imagine and more entangled than we can conceive.

Goethe, *If Ignorance Is Bliss, Why Aren't There More Happy People?*

❖ ❖ ❖

It's not the will to win that matters—everyone has that. It's the will to prepare to win that matters.

Paul "Bear" Bryant

❖ ❖ ❖

By failing to prepare you are preparing to fail.

Benjamin Franklin

❖ ❖ ❖

Do I Patiently Manage My Team's Development Through the Predictable Stages?

Similar to a child, a team goes through several stages of development. The four major stages of team development include:

Forming. The first stage in a team's development, forming is characterized by unclear expectations, hesitant participation, and suspicion among its members.

Storming. . . . is characterized by in-fighting, defensiveness, and competition.

Norming. . . . is characterized by cohesiveness, intimacy, and establishment of personal norms.

Performing. . . . is characterized by effective problem solving and decision making.

Kimberly Mullins, *Lessons in Teamwork*, 1995

❖ ❖ ❖

Spend lots of time together. Common sense tells us that teams must spend a lot of time together, especially at the beginning. Yet potential teams often fail to do so.

Jon R. Katzenbach and Douglas K. Smith, "The Wisdom of Teams", *Harper Business*, 1993

❖ ❖ ❖

Teams go through a number of stages in their development. The length and complexity of each stage is a function of the complexity of the goals and assignment of the team, as well as the number and personal style of the team members. The following . . . describes the stages of the process for creating a high performance team.

Forming/Chartering (definition, purpose, responsibilities, operating guidelines, endorsement)

Norming/Developing (decision-making, problem-solving, process improvement, tools, interpersonal behaviors)

Excelling/Sustaining (feedback, measurement, self-correction, continuous improvement)

Paul Plotczyck, Richard Jones, and Paul Stimson, *Linkage, Inc.'s Best Practices in Teams Guidebook,* 2000

❖ ❖ ❖

By choosing a team path instead of the working group, people commit to take the risks of conflict, joint work-products, and collective action necessary to build a common purpose, set of goals, approach, and mutual accountability. People who call themselves teams but take no such risks are at best pseudo-teams. Potential teams that take the risks to climb the curve inevitably confront obstacles. Some teams overcome them; others get stuck. The worst thing a stuck team can to, however, is to abandon the discipline of team basics. . . . Performance, not team building, can save potential teams or pseudo-teams, no matter how stuck.

Jon R. Katzenbach and Douglas K. Smith, "The Wisdom of Teams", *Harper Business*, 1993

❖ ❖ ❖

The middle of every successful project looks like a disaster.

Rosabeth Moss Cantor

❖ ❖ ❖

Anything worth doing does not have to be done perfectly—at first.

Managers should recognize that good performance, both their own and others, is a journey, not a destination. Everyone learns by doing. It takes time and practice to achieve specific goals.

For example, the managers who attend my training seminars often get very excited by some of the concepts they learn. They return to their organizations all fired up about using a new idea or approach. However, when people don't respond immediately as anticipated, they often become discouraged and abandon the concept, deciding that it doesn't work.

It's counterproductive to be too hard on yourself. Don't expect instant perfection. While self-criticism is healthy, it should not be destructive. It's unfair to be hard on yourself the first time you attempt something new. It is also unfair to expect such an unrealistic standard from others. It's not necessary to do everything exactly right the first time.

Ken Blanchard, *The Heart of a Leader*

❖ ❖ ❖

The test of good management is whether it enables the successful performer to do her work.

Peter F. Drucker, "The Practice of Management", *The Daily Drucker*

❖ ❖ ❖

Do I Lead in Executing Plans and Goals?

Seventy percent of strategic failures are due to poor execution…
it's rarely for lack of smarts or vision.

Ram Charan, coauthor of *Execution: The Discipline of Getting Things Done*

❖ ❖ ❖

Organizational leaders can foster team performance best by building a strong performance ethic rather than by establishing a team-promoting environment. In fact, too many executives fall into the trap of appearing to promote teams for the sake of teams. Real teams are much more likely to flourish if leaders aim their sights on performance results that balance the needs of customers, employees, and shareholders.

Jon R. Katzenbach and Douglas K. Smith, "The Wisdom of Teams*", Harper Business*, 1993

❖ ❖ ❖

Delay is the deadliest form of denial.

C. Northcote Parkinson

❖ ❖ ❖

It's one thing to come up with great strategies and goals; it's quite another to actually get them done. This is what we call the execution gap The execution gap is the great unaddressed issue today in the business world. Eighty percent of the results come from twenty percent of the activities. Many people regard execution as detail work that's beneath the dignity of a business leader. That's wrong…it's a leader's most important job.

Ram Charan, coauthor of *Execution: The Discipline of Getting Things Done*

❖ ❖ ❖

A key to execution of goals is to possess the ability to carry out worthwhile behaviors and decisions after the emotion of making the commitment has passed.

Hyrum Smith

❖ ❖ ❖

Execution is the great unaddressed issue in the business world today. Its absence is the single biggest obstacle to success and the cause of most of the disappointments that are mistakenly attributed to other causes.

Ram Charan, *Execution: the Discipline of Getting Things Done*

❖ ❖ ❖

The disciplines of execution is a systematic way of **exposing reality** and **acting on it**. Most organizations don't face reality very well...that's the basic reason they have a difficult time focusing on and executing their key goals.

Larry Bossidy & Ram Charan, *Execution: The Discipline of Getting Things Done*

❖ ❖ ❖

If you can execute, you can accomplish anything. When a company has a clear mission, strategy, and goals and people know how their individual mission fits into the big picture -- everyone paddles in the same direction.

Stephen Cooper

❖ ❖ ❖

What Is Great Execution? The discipline of getting the most important things done, amidst all the other competing priorities of the whirlwind. Leaders who concentrate on effective execution find that they and their teams actually accomplish more by focusing on less--and that is liberating and empowering for both the leaders and their teams.

Michael Simpson

❖ ❖ ❖

Strategy gets you on the playing field, but execution pays the bills.

Gordon Eubanks

❖ ❖ ❖

Key goals must be communicated again and again, emphasized over and over, and progress tracked visibly and continually.

Stephen R. Covey, "Knowledge Workers in the Dark," *Execution Essentials*

❖ ❖ ❖

The top 10 global issues by CEO's and leadership teams boil down to two key issues. One, excellence in execution of teams. Two, consistent execution of strategy by top management.

The Conference Board, Global CEO Challenge Survey, *Financial Crisis Edition*, 2008,09,10

❖ ❖ ❖

65

When all of these 4 Disciplines of Execution (Discipline 1: Goal clarity of the most critically important, Discipline 2: The right weekly actions to drive the goal to completion, Discipline 3: Keeping score and knowing if you are winning or losing each week, Discipline 4: Hold teams and individuals accountable each week.) are practiced, the chances of successful execution go up dramatically. But when even one discipline is missing or deficient, the chances of successful execution plummets.

Execution Essentials

❖ ❖ ❖

Follow through is the cornerstone of execution and every leader who's good at executing follows through religiously. Following through ensures that people are doing the things they committed to do.

Larry Bossidy

❖ ❖ ❖

You hear it—you know. You see it—you understand.
When you do it—you remember.

Confucius

❖ ❖ ❖

Potential is always blocked by interference. And interference is reduced or eliminated by focus. The challenge is to manage our interference by finding a dependable, systemized way to create focus. Focused attention can improve performance in any areas of life.

Alan Fine

❖ ❖ ❖

We have a passion for winning in everything we do. We focus on hiring great people, innovating on our core processes, and delivering great results.

Michael Dell

❖ ❖ ❖

We must all suffer from one of two pains: the pain of discipline or the pain of regret.

Jim Rohn

❖ ❖ ❖

Leadership without the discipline of execution is both incomplete and ineffective.

Ram Charan

❖ ❖ ❖

Without the ability to execute on a few key priorities all other attributes of leadership become hollow.

Larry Bossidy Chairman,

❖ ❖ ❖

Great organizations, like great racing teams, have an execution system that ensures the predictability of results.

Robert Kaplan and David Norton, *The Balanced Scorecard*

❖ ❖ ❖

People who get ahead are those who prove they can get things done.

David Kearns

❖ ❖ ❖

The best discipline, maybe the only discipline that really works, is self-discipline.

Walter Kiechel III, *Fortune Magazine*

❖ ❖ ❖

You can craft elegant strategies, but if you can't implement them and you don't have the tenacity to follow through on them you're not worth anything. If you look at companies that have done really well, they have great strategies, but more important, they have focused execution.

Kevin Rollins

❖ ❖ ❖

Many people regard execution as detail work that's beneath the dignity of a business leader. That's wrong. To the contrary, it's a leader's most important job.

Larry Bossidy and Ram Charan, *Execution: The Discipline of Getting Things Done*

❖ ❖ ❖

Whenever a new goal is set, someone somewhere must do something they've never done before; and until they do that, there is no execution. They must change their behavior. And changing behavior is perhaps the hardest thing we ever do—which goes a long way toward explaining why most organizations suffer from an execution gap.
Defining and acting on the right weekly or daily lead measures gives us enormous freedom, partly because it ensures that the real work is aligned with the goal, and is not just "hard work." In a way, lead measures enable us to work "smarter" rather than just "harder."

Execution Essentials

❖ ❖ ❖

Nothing big gets accomplished in one day. Resolutions are set in one day, but accomplished with a hundred tiny steps that happen throughout the year. New Year's resolutions should be nothing more than a starting point. You must develop a ritual or habit for revisiting your plan. *myGoals.com*

For the purposes of action, nothing is more useful than narrowness of thought combined with energy of will.

Henri-Frederic Amiel

❖ ❖ ❖

No company can deliver on its commitment or adapt well to change unless all leaders practice the discipline of execution at all levels. Execution has to be a part of a company's strategy and its goals. It is the missing link between aspirations and results. As such, it is a major—indeed, *the* major—job of a business leader. If you don't know how to execute, the whole of your effort as a leader will always be less than the sum of its parts.

Larry Bossidy and Ram Charan, *Execution: The Discipline of Getting Things Done*

❖ ❖ ❖

Putting an execution environment in place is hard, but losing it is easy.

Larry Bossidy and Ram Charan, *Execution: The Discipline of Getting Things Done*

❖ ❖ ❖

Everyone wants to win. Everyone wants to make a contribution that matters. But too many organizations lack this kind of discipline—the conscious, consistent regimen needed to execute key goals with excellence. The cost to the organization of a failure to execute pales in comparison to the human cost to people who want to give their best. By contrast, nothing is more motivating than belonging to a team of people who know the goal and are determined to get there.

Execution Essentials

❖ ❖ ❖

90 percent of managers are typically either distracted or disengaged from key organizational objectives......confusing frenetic motion with constructive action, they are noted for their unproductive busyness.

Heike Bruch and Sumantra Ghoshal

❖ ❖ ❖

Very few managers use their time effectively. They may think they're attending to pressing matters, but they are really just spinning their wheels and producing unproductive busyness. The key to effectiveness is having a high degree of purpose, but only about 10 percent of managers show that trait.

Heike Bruch and Sumantra Ghoshal

❖ ❖ ❖

Execution is the great unaddressed issue in the business world today. Its absence is the single biggest obstacle to success and the cause of most of the disappointments that are mistakenly attributed to other causes.

Ram Charan, *Execution: the Discipline of Getting Things Done*

❖ ❖ ❖

In order for leaders and teams to significantly raise performance and results, Leaders need to co-create high level goals and expectations with team members while helping them understand each member's commitment level. Leaders must trust the team members, hold them accountable weekly to their most important commitments, plan future weekly commitments, and re-engaging them around performance targets and measures that are easily tracked on visible, compelling, player-level scoreboards.

Michael Simpson, FranklinCovey

❖ ❖ ❖

I've never met a person I considered competent who didn't follow through. I bet it's the same for you. Willa A. Foster remarked, "Quality is never an accident; it is always the result of high intention, sincere effort, intelligent direction and skillful execution; it represents the wise choice of many alternatives."

Performing at a high level of excellence is always a choice, an act of the will. As leaders, we expect our people to follow through when we hand them the ball. They expect that and a whole lot more from us as their leaders.

John C. Maxwell, *The 21 Indispensable Qualities of a Leader*

❖ ❖ ❖

Apathy can only be overcome by enthusiasm, and enthusiasm can only be aroused by two things: First, an ideal that takes the imagination by storm; second, a definite, intelligible plan for carrying that ideal into practice.

Arnold Toynbee, *Everyday Greatness,* by Stephen R. Covey

❖ ❖ ❖

Take time to deliberate, but when the time for action
has arrived, stop thinking and go in.

Napoleon Bonaparte

❖ ❖ ❖

High performers:

Maintain high standards of performance

Set measurable standards of excellence for themselves and others

Promote a spirit of continuous improvement

Poor performers:

Fail to build high commitment among all employees to team goals and objectives

John H. Zenger and Joseph Folkman, *The Extraordinary Leader*

❖ ❖ ❖

The great successful men (women) of the world have used their imagination...
They think ahead and create their mental picture, and then go to work
materializing that picture in all its details, filling in here, adding a little
there, altering this a bit and that a bit, but steadily building—steadily building.

Robert Collier

❖ ❖ ❖

It is always true that we intend to do many things we never get around to doing.
There may be many reasons for this. Sometimes we sit and wait for supposedly
ideal conditions. But the so-called ideal conditions rarely come. If the men who
have most enriched the world had waited for the ideal conditions before
beginning their work, we should have had few inventions, few masterworks, few
discoveries. Men have written and painted, thought and planned, worked and
searched, often in poverty, sometimes in illness, frequently in unsympathetic
surroundings—against hunger, against discouragement, against
misunderstanding. There rarely comes a
time in the life of any man when all difficulty, all distraction, and all
annoyance are removed. The postponement, the putting off, that always
waits for supposedly better times and circumstances, that always
waits for ideal conditions, may be the postponement that steals away life itself.

Richard L. Evans

❖ ❖ ❖

Keeping Score: Do I Fairly and Effectively Measure Performance?

You have to know where you stand and where you want to go, or else it isn't going to happen. Numbers bring clarity.

Subir Chowdhury, *Execution Essentials*

❖ ❖ ❖

What gets measured, gets managed...what gets managed gets done,

Peter F. Drucker

❖ ❖ ❖

People play differently when they start to keep score.

Chris McChesney

❖ ❖ ❖

The fundamental purpose of the scoreboard is to motivate the players to win.

Jim Stuart

❖ ❖ ❖

Give full measure, when you measure and weigh with even scales. That is fair and better in the end.

Surah 55: Ayah 9

❖ ❖ ❖

High performers:

Take personal responsibility for outcomes

Can be counted on to follow through on commitments

Go above and beyond what needs to be done without being told

Poor performers:

Blame failures on others

Lose interest before projects are completed and fail to follow through

John H. Zenger and Joseph Folkman, *The Extraordinary Leader*

❖ ❖ ❖

Protecting underperformers always backfires.

Jack Welch

❖ ❖ ❖

No goal can be operationalized until measurable criteria have been developed. Without measures, goals are lofty statements of intent, but do not drive behavior or create focus and direction.

Paul Plotczyck, Richard Jones, and Paul Stimson, *Linkage, Inc.'s Best Practices in Teams Guidebook* , 2000

❖ ❖ ❖

In God we trust, everyone else data.

Mahan Khalsa

❖ ❖ ❖

Some of the most effective managers I know go one step further. They have each of their subordinate's write a "managers letter" twice a year. In this letter to his superior, each manager first defines the objectives of his superior's job and of his own job as he sees them. He then sets down the performance standards, which he believes are being applied to him. Next, he lists the things he must do himself to attain these goals—and the things within his own unit he considers to be the major obstacles. He lists the things his superior and the company do that help him and the things that hamper him. Finally, he outlines what he proposes to do during the next year to reach his goals. If his superior accepts this statement, the "managers' letter" becomes the charter under which the manager operates.

Peter Drucker, "The Practice of Management",

Harper Business, 1954,1984

❖ ❖ ❖

Focusing on the right work and the right measures is the key role of a leader in any organization.

Ram Charan

❖ ❖ ❖

People disengage from a goal for three reasons: 1. They don't know what game they are playing. 2. They don't know the score, 3. They don't know what they need to do each week that can affect the score.

Chris McChesney

❖ ❖ ❖

Some of the most important things in life are unknowable and un-measureable.

Albert Einstein

❖ ❖ ❖

Leaders will minimize fear and uncertainty by motivating their team members to win by focusing on the right goals with a clear, visible scoreboard that showcases what each person can do each week to best impact the score.

Michael K. Simpson

❖ ❖ ❖

We have found that by identifying, monitoring, tracking the right weekly lead behaviors, these proactive actions change behavior faster than any other effort. Once identified, team members now have a clear map of the best-practice behaviors that driving goal achievement.

Michael K. Simpson

❖ ❖ ❖

Scoreboards can be a constructive leadership tool to help focus, motivate, and inspire team members around a winnable game.

Jim Huling

❖ ❖ ❖

When scoreboards are developed they should feel a little like a game...leaders should work together with the team members to help their monitor results in a way that helps the player engage in the game each and every week.

Chris McChesney

❖ ❖ ❖

We have found that too often people don't know whether they are winning or losing in the workplace, until monthly or quarterly financial results are posted. That's too late for course correction. The key is to balance the focus between both the lag measures and the leading actions that the players do each week to drive performance.

Chris McChesney

❖ ❖ ❖

The truth is more important than the facts.

Frank Lloyd Wright

❖ ❖ ❖

People disengage from work when: 1. They don't know what they will be judged or how they will be evaluated for successful performance. 2. They don't know if they are winning or losing at work. 3. They don't know what they do each week that will directly impact the score on their successful performance.

Execution Essentials

❖ ❖ ❖

The spider-web of facts, many a truth is strangled

Paul Eldridge

❖ ❖ ❖

The facts are our friends.

Paul Gustavson

❖ ❖ ❖

In God we trust, everyone else data.

Mahan Khalsa

❖ ❖ ❖

Facts are the enemy of truth.

Miguel Cervantes

❖ ❖ ❖

Do not become a mere recorder of facts, but try to penetrate the mystery of their origin.

Ivan Petrovich Pavlov

❖ ❖ ❖

Anyone who is practically acquainted with scientific work is aware that those who refuse to go beyond the facts rarely get as far as fact.

Sir Arthur Conan Doyle

❖ ❖ ❖

There are no facts, only interpretations.

Freidrich Nietzsche

❖ ❖ ❖

Do I Establish a Positive Team Culture?

You cannot be a truly effective leader, the kind that people *want* to follow, unless you love people. Physicist Albert Einstein put it this way, "Strange is our situation here upon earth. Each of us comes for a short visit, not knowing why, yet sometimes seeming to divine a purpose. From the standpoint of daily life, however, there is one thing we do know: that man is here for the sake of other men."

John C. Maxwell, *The 21 Indispensable Qualities of a Leader*

❖ ❖ ❖

Coming together is a beginning; keeping together is progress; working together is success.

Henry Ford, *Everyday Greatness,* by Stephen R. Covey

❖ ❖ ❖

Behavior is a culmination of common, consistent, and observable actions that people do every day.

David Hanna

❖ ❖ ❖

Do I Promote True Interdependence?

This is how high performing teams function. They are clear about their collective responsibility. They are also clear about the individual responsibility of each team member, and make sure that they collectively meet or exceed the team requirements. They play their own positions with an eye on how their teammates are doing as well. As required, team members extend their roles and support each other. They realize that the failure of any team member to fulfill a personal responsibility will lead to the failure of the entire team. The high performing team plays the entire field, and ensures that all individual and collective responsibilities are covered at all times.

Paul Plotczyck, Richard Jones, and Paul Stimson, *Linkage, Inc.'s Best Practices in Teams Guidebook,* 2000

❖ ❖ ❖

In order for a team to achieve synergistic results, there are some "rules of conduct" that must be followed. If these rules are violated, they can both create disruptive behavior and cause the team to become dysfunctional. For this reason, a team should examine these behaviors, modify or add to them as appropriate for its circumstances, and then monitor its behavior against these behavioral rules. . .
.

Team goals are the highest priority—not individual or personal goals.

Check your job at the door—no "positional" behavior.

Decisions are based on what's right—not who's right.

Everyone has the responsibility to both contribute and listen to the contributions of others—there is no inequality in the team.

Contribute with flexibility—no fixed positions.

Consensus prevails—the right of "infinite refusal" is not acceptable.

Decisions are based on facts and analysis—not opinion management.

Decisions are made in real time—not at "off-line" negotiations.

Perfection can be the enemy of the good—the 80-20 rule prevails.

The team should strive for consensus—not unanimity.

Paul Plotczyck, Richard Jones, and Paul Stimson, *Linkage, Inc.'s Best Practices in Teams Guidebook,* 2000

❖ ❖ ❖

Cooperation is the thorough conviction that nobody can get
there unless everybody gets there.

Virginia Burden

❖ ❖ ❖

Self-preservation and individual accountability can work two ways. Left
unattended, they can preclude or destroy potential teams. But recognized and
addressed for what they are, especially if done with reference to how to meet a
performance challenge, individual concerns and differences become a source of
collective strength. Teams are not antithetical to individual performance. Real
teams always find ways for each individual to contribute and thereby gain
distinction. Indeed, when harnessed to a common team purpose and goals, our
need to distinguish ourselves as individuals becomes a powerful engine for
performance.

Jon R. Katzenbach and Douglas K. Smith, "The Wisdom of Teams", *Harper
Business*, 1993

❖ ❖ ❖

If everyone is thinking alike, then somebody isn't thinking.

George S. Patton

❖ ❖ ❖

Snowflakes are one of nature's most fragile things, but just look at
what they can do when they stick together.

Vesta Kelly

❖ ❖ ❖

Truly the faithful are to one another like components of a building—
each part supports the other.

Muslim and Bukhari

❖ ❖ ❖

No man is an island, entire of itself; every man is a piece of continent, a part of
the main. If a clod be washed away by the sea, Europe is the less, as well as if a
promontory were, as well as if a manor of thy friend's or of thine own were: any
man's death diminishes me, because I am involved in mankind, and
therefore never send to know for whom the bell tolls; it tolls for thee.

John Donne

❖ ❖ ❖

Great men are rarely isolated mountain peaks; they are the summits of ranges.

T.W. Higginson

❖ ❖ ❖

It is thus that man, who can subsist only in society, was fitted by nature to that situation for which he made all members of human society stand in need of each other's assistance, and are likewise exposed to mutual injuries. Where the necessary assistance is reciprocally afforded from love, from gratitude, from friendship and esteem, the society flourishes and is happy. All the different members of it are bound together by the agreeable bands of love and affection, and are, as it were, drawn to one common centre of mutual good offices.

Adam Smith, *Moral Sentiments*

❖ ❖ ❖

Adam Smith's point was that people could conduct business on a minimal level as long as there was a critical amount of "intentional virtue" in the society. So they may be after their own self- interest, but not at the expense of others by stealing or cheating. However, for a society to prosper this "intentional virtue" and moral character would need to be abundant. Competition was good in society to improve performance, provide self-determination, and increase performance and results. The key is for competition not to be destructive or as long as it was not abused in the sole pursuit of money and wealth without moral virtue and regard for the society as a whole.

It is not the love of our neighbour, it is not the love of mankind, which upon many occasions prompts us to the practice of those divine virtues. It is a stronger love, a more powerful affection, which generally takes place upon such occasions: the love of what is honourable and noble, of the grandeur, and dignity, and superiority of our own character.

Adam Smith, *Moral Sentiments*

❖ ❖ ❖

There is really no such creature as a single individual; he has no more life of his own than a cast-off cell marooned from the surface of your skin.

Lewis Thomas, *Healing After Loss*

❖ ❖ ❖

In the ethics of interdependence there are only obligations, and all obligations are mutual obligations. Harmony and trust—that is, interdependence—require that each side be obligated to provide what the other side needs to achieve its goals and to fulfill itself.

Peter F. Drucker, "The Changing World of the Executive",
The Manager's Book of Quotations

❖ ❖ ❖

The wish to be independent of all men, and not to be under obligation to any one is the sure sign of a soul without tenderness.

Joseph Joubert, "Thoughts", *The Manager's Book of Quotations*

❖ ❖ ❖

"We" rather than "I."

Charles Garfield, "Peak Performers", *The Manager's Book of Quotations*

❖ ❖ ❖

I'm naturally a delegator. I guess I realized early in life that, unless you're going to be a violinist or something, your success will probably depend on other people.

William G. McGowan, *Inc. Magazine,* August 1986, *The Manager's Book of* Quotations

❖ ❖ ❖

One day a small boy tried to lift a heavy stone, but couldn't budge it. His father, watching, finally said, "Are you sure you're using all your strength?"

"Yes, I am!" the boy cried.

❖ ❖ ❖

"No you're not," said the father. "You haven't asked me to help you."

Bits & Pieces

❖ ❖ ❖

No member of a crew is praised for the rugged individuality of his rowing.

Ralph Waldo Emerson

❖ ❖ ❖

Light is the task where many share the toil.

Homer

❖ ❖ ❖

Do I Foster Relationships of Trust?

Trust is the one thing as a leader that impacts everything you do.

Stephen R. Covey

❖ ❖ ❖

What is trust? I could give you a dictionary definition, but you know it when you feel it. Trust happens when leaders are transparent, candid, and keep their word. It's that simple.

Jack Welch

❖ ❖ ❖

To deeply understand another's point of view, and to be able to explain that point of view as well as or better than he or she could. To be open and see someone's differences as worthwhile.

Author Unknown

❖ ❖ ❖

We should place confidence in our employee. Confidence is the foundation of friendship. If we give it, we will receive it. Any person in a managerial position, from supervisor to president, who feels that his employee is basically not as good as he is and who suspects his employee is always trying to put something over on him, lacks the necessary qualities for human leadership—to say nothing of human friendship.

Harry E. Humphreys, Jr., *Thoughts On Leadership*

❖ ❖ ❖

Real teams do not emerge unless the individuals on them take risks involving conflict, trust, interdependence, and hard work. Of the risks required, the most formidable involve building the trust and interdependence necessary to move from individual accountability to mutual accountability. People on real teams must trust and depend on one another—not totally or forever—but certainly with respect to the team's purpose, performance goals, and approach. For most of us such trust and interdependence do not come easily; it must be earned and demonstrated repeatedly if it is to change behavior.

Jon R. Katzenbach and Douglas K. Smith, "The Wisdom of Teams", *Harper Business*, 1993

❖ ❖ ❖

Effective, long-term relationships require mutual respect and mutual benefit.

Stephen R. Covey

❖ ❖ ❖

Give trust conditionally, but always be unconditionally trustworthy.

When trust is high, speed is fast and costs are low;

When trust is low, speed is slow and costs are high.

Stephen MR Covey

❖ ❖ ❖

Unexpressed feelings never die; they are buried alive and come forth in uglier ways.

Stephen R.Covey

❖ ❖ ❖

Most people listen not with the intent to understand, but with the intent to reply.

Stephen R. Covey

❖ ❖ ❖

To be with another empathically means that for the time being, you lay aside your own views and values in order to enter another's world without prejudice. In a sense you lay aside yourself; this can only be done by people that are secure in themselves.

Carl Rogers

❖ ❖ ❖

You listen with your ears, but you hear with your heart and your mind.

Arabic Saying

❖ ❖ ❖

You may be deceived if you trust too much, but you will live in torment if you do not trust enough.

Frank Crane

❖ ❖ ❖

Trust becomes a verb when you communicate to others their worth and potential so clearly that they are inspired to see it in themselves.

Stephen R. Covey

❖ ❖ ❖

To be trusted is a greater compliment than being loved.

George MacDonald

❖ ❖ ❖

To trust life, you have to trust others; and to trust others, you have to trust yourself.

The Bhagavad Gita

❖ ❖ ❖

The low trust leader believes that "I simply talk the talk." The high trust leader believes that "I not only walk the talk but walk the walk." The best way to influence others is through being credible, rather than to pretend to be trustworthy or to simply say so. Trust always starts first with me. How am I showing up as a leader? As a leader, am I seeking to model trustworthy behaviors? Am I seeking to be a fundamentally trustworthy person?

Stephen MR Covey

❖ ❖ ❖

What you do speaks more loudly than what you say.

Quaker Proverb

❖ ❖ ❖

One who doesn't really trust himself can never really trust anyone else.

Jean-Francois de Gondi

❖ ❖ ❖

It is better to trust once in a while and be disappointed than to distrust and be disappointed all the time.

Abraham Lincoln

❖ ❖ ❖

Even in difficult situations in close, personal or customer relationships, trust can be restored. And the very effort of restoring trust can make it strong than before.

Stephen R. Covey

❖ ❖ ❖

Trust everybody, but cut the cards.

Finley Peter Dunne

❖ ❖ ❖

We cannot talk our way out of problems that we behaved ourselves into. However, we can behave ourselves out of problems and improve trust in a short time than most think possible.

Stephen MR Covey

❖ ❖ ❖

Confidence is the foundation for all business relations. The degree of confidence one person has for another determines their standing in the commercial and business world.

William JH Boetcker

❖ ❖ ❖

The high trust leader does not say that trust starts with you. The high trust leader believes that trust always starts with me first. Like a ripple effect in a pond my trust is a functions of improving two key aspects: First, my character, which is my integrity and intent. Second, is my competence, my capabilities and results. Anyone can be a high trust leader as they increase both character and competence.

Stephen R. Covey

❖ ❖ ❖

In today's competitive environment, some leaders are tempted to abandon ethical considerations. Somehow they think that playing by the rule of "anything goes" is going to win for them.
These leaders are jeopardizing far more than they imagine. First of all, they stand to lose respect. The number one characteristic employees say they are looking for in a leader is integrity. They also risk losing repeat customers and competent people. You can make a quick financial gain by taking advantage of your customers or your people, but the loss of trust may never be restored. The third thing they are placing at risk is their own self-esteem.

Ken Blanchard, The Heart of a Leader

❖ ❖ ❖

False scales are an abomination to the Lord; But a just weight is his delight.

Proverbs 11:1

❖ ❖ ❖

In three ways is a wise man known: By his dealings with his fellow man, by his quickness in granting pardon, and his love of all people. The fool is known in three ways: By his quickness to answer, his volubility, and his faith in all people.

Joseph ibn Zabara, "The Book of Delight", *The Manager's Book of Quotations*

❖ ❖ ❖

Leadership is the capacity and will to rally men and women to a common purpose and the character which inspires confidence.

Bernard Montgomery, *The 21 Indispensable Qualities of a Leader*

❖ ❖ ❖

Leadership is not something you do *to* people. It's something you do *with* people.

Ken Blanchard, Patricia Zigarmi, and Drea Zigarmi, *Leadership and the One Minute Manager*

❖ ❖ ❖

Invest in the Emotional Bank Account of that person. The Emotional Bank Account is the amount of trust in the relationship. Withdrawals break down trust. Make deposits. Describe three things you think the person would consider a deposit and do them—repeatedly. Deposits include acknowledgment of good performance, honest feedback, an apology, or just sitting down and listening to the person.

Avoid making withdrawals. Identify three things you think the person would consider withdrawals, and avoid doing them.

Be patient. A quick fix is a mirage. Building and repairing relationships takes time, and showing impatience is a huge withdrawal.

Franklin Covey, *Management Essentials*

❖ ❖ ❖

People who are able to help others soothe their feelings have an especially valued social commodity; they are the souls others turn to when in greatest emotional need. We are all part of each other's tool kit for emotional change, for better or for worse.

Daniel Goleman, *Emotional Intelligence*

❖ ❖ ❖

A man whose *word* will not inform you at all what he means or will do, is not a man you can bargain with. You must get out of that man's way, or put him out of yours!

Thomas Carlyle, "On Heroes and Hero-Worship", *The Manager's Book of Quotations*

❖ ❖ ❖

The chief lesson I have learned in a long life is that the only way you can make a man trustworthy is by trusting him; and the surest way to make him untrustworthy is to distrust him and show your distrust.

Henry L. Stimpson, Memo to President Franklin Delano Roosevelt, September 1945, *The Manager's Book of Quotations*

❖ ❖ ❖

To work effectively and successfully in what is increasingly a team- or alliance-based environment, we must be trusted. It is hard to trust someone who is always thinking of himself or herself first. It is much easier to trust someone who is focused outward and sensitive to the needs of others. Consequently, pride is not only unattractive, but it will increasingly get in the way of personal effectiveness and success. By their very nature, teams and alliances require sharing, giving, helping trusting—the very opposite of the selfishness of pride.

Mark H. Willes, *Business with Integrity*

❖ ❖ ❖

Few things help an individual more than to place responsibility upon him and to let him know that you trust him.

Booker T. Washington, *If Ignorance Is Bliss, Why Aren't There More Happy People?*

❖ ❖ ❖

Organizations are no longer built on force. They are increasingly built on trust. And this presupposes that people understand one another.

Peter Drucker, *Management Essentials*

❖ ❖ ❖

The power is detested, and miserable the life, of him who wishes to be feared rather than to be loved.

Cornelius Nepos

❖ ❖ ❖

How do I build trusting relationships with my team?
Build trust by making deposits in the "Emotional Bank Accounts" of the people you work with.

Clarify your expectations of them so there are no misunderstandings

Acknowledge good performance. Make it a habit.

Give and receive honest, accurate feedback.

Keep your commitment or explain why you can't.

Be loyal to the absent. Don't talk about people behind their backs.

Apologize sincerely when you make a "withdrawal"

Listen empathically (Habit 5) to their concern.

Franklin Covey, *Management Essentials*

❖ ❖ ❖

He makes a great mistake ... who supposes that authority is firmer or better established when it is founded by force than that which is welded by affection.

Terence

❖ ❖ ❖

Team player: Once who unites others toward a shared destiny through sharing information and ideas, empowering others and developing trust.

Dennis Kinlaw

❖ ❖ ❖

Smart people instinctively understand the dangers of entrusting our future to self-serving leaders who use our institutions, whether in the corporate or social sectors, to advance their own interests.

Jim Collins

❖ ❖ ❖

Trust is rebuilt by focusing not on what the other person did or did not do but on critiquing one's own behavior, improving one's trustworthiness, and focusing attention not on words and promises but on actions, attitudes, and ways of being.

Kenneth Cloke and Joan Goldsmith

❖ ❖ ❖

When a gifted team dedicates itself to unselfish trust and combines
instinct with boldness and effort, it is ready to climb.

Patanjali, Ancient Yoga Master

❖ ❖ ❖

It's a vice to trust everyone, and equally a vice to trust no one.

Seneca

❖ ❖ ❖

Men of genius are admired, men of wealth are envied, men of power
are feared, but only men of character are trusted.

Zig Ziglar

❖ ❖ ❖

The glue that holds all relationships together—including the relationship
between the leader and the led—is trust, and trust is based on integrity.

Brian Tracy

❖ ❖ ❖

The chief lesson I have learned in a long life is that the only way
to make a man trustworthy is to trust him.

Henry Stimson

❖ ❖ ❖

I have found that by trusting people until they prove themselves
unworthy of that trust, a lot more happens.

Jim Burke

❖ ❖ ❖

People ask me how I've had the interest and zeal to hang in there and do what
I've done. I say, "Because my father treated me with very stern discipline: he
trusted me. I'm stuck, I've got to see the trust through." He trusted me. I trust
other people. And they did the job.

Robert Galvin, Jr.

❖ ❖ ❖

How Well Do I Listen to Others?

I make progress by having people around who are smarter than I am—and listening to them. And I assume that everyone is smarter about something than I am.

Henry J. Kaiser

❖ ❖ ❖

The greatest gift you can give another is the purity of your attention.

Richard Moss, M.D

❖ ❖ ❖

We are often stunned to see the number of people in middle management positions in organizations who lack the most rudimentary of social skills. These basic human skills include:

When you talk to people, look them in the eye.

Learn and use people's names.

When talking with people, say or do things that let the other person know you are listening and understanding.

Do not dominate the conversation and take all the "air time."

Sincerely inquire about others' ideas and activities.

Laugh at others' jokes and attempts at humor.

Praise others' hard work and efforts in furthering a good cause.

Smile when meeting and greeting other people

John H. Zenger and Joseph Folkman, *The Extraordinary Leader*

❖ ❖ ❖

How can you have charisma? Be more concerned about making others feel good about themselves than you are making them feel good about you.

Dan Reiland

❖ ❖ ❖

Greatness is defined by the Savior as the servant: "...the same is appointed to be the greatest, notwithstanding he is the least and the servant of all."

Stephen R. Covey, *Business with Integrity*

❖ ❖ ❖

Nothing is worse than active ignorance.

Johann Wolfgang von Goethe, *Goethe's World View Presented in His Reflections and Maxims*

❖ ❖ ❖

There is a profound difference between information and meaning.

Warren G. Bennis, University of Maryland symposium, January 21, 1988, The Manager's Book of Quotations

❖ ❖ ❖

Listen. Don't explain or justify.

William G. Dyer, "Strategies for Managing Change", *The Manager's Book of Quotations*

❖ ❖ ❖

Unfortunately, most of us listen through a screen of resistance. We are screened with prejudices, whether religious or spiritual, psychological or scientific; or, with daily worries, desire, and fears. And with these fears for a screen, we listen. Therefore we listen really to our own noise, our own sound, not to what is being said.

Jiddu Krishnamurti, "The First and Last Freedom", *The Manager's Book of Quotations*

❖ ❖ ❖

Be a good listener. Unlike your mouth, your ears will never get you in trouble.

Frank Tyger, *If Ignorance Is Bliss, Why Aren't There More Happy People?*

❖ ❖ ❖

The word "listen" contains the same letters as the word "silent."

Alfred Brendel, *Everyday Greatness,* by Stephen R. Covey

❖ ❖ ❖

Deeply listening is miraculous for both listener and speaker. When someone welcomes us with open-hearted, accepting, interested listening, our spirits expand and we are inspired to unveil the miracle of our Self.

The Yiddish proverb "There is no one as deaf as he who will not listen" speaks simply to a basic truth. We have an epidemic of deafness in our world, and the result of not hearing one another in a meaningful way is a profound and poignant loneliness. As plants shrivel without sun and water, we are dying in spirit for lack of deep listening.   The words *heart* and *listen* provide hints about the art of listening deeply. *Heart* contains within it the word *hear*, and *listen* contains the exact same letters as *silent*. In order to hear what is being said and felt, we need to be silent and listen from our hearts, we must close our mouths and give undivided attention to others when they open theirs.

Sue Patton Thoele, *Woman's Book of Soul*

❖ ❖ ❖

How do I listen empathically?

Listen when you need to truly understand the concerns of an employee, an associate, your boss, a customer, or a supplier:

Don't agree, disagree, judge, probe, or advise. Those responses come later.

Reflect content. Put the meaning of the person's words in your own words.

Reflect feeling. Concentrate on and echo the other person's feeling.

Respond like this when listening empathically:

--It sounds like you feel_____ about _____.

--So you are saying _____.

--I'm really trying to understand. Are you saying_____.

Franklin Covey, *Management Essentials*

❖ ❖ ❖

If managers are careless about basic things—telling the truth, respecting moral codes, proper professional conduct—who can believe them on other issues?

James L. Hayes, "Memos for Management: Leadership", *The Manager's Book of Quotations*

❖ ❖ ❖

The most important thing in communication is hearing what isn't said.

Peter Drucker

❖ ❖ ❖

High performers:

Are trusted by work group members

Balance concern for productivity and results with sensitivity for employees' needs/problems

Are approachable and friendly

Poor performers:

Are difficult to get along with

People don't feel free to take their complaints to them,

John H. Zenger and Joseph Folkman, *The Extraordinary Leader*

❖ ❖ ❖

Le Roy H. Kurtz of General motors said, "The fields of industry are strewn with the bones of those organizations whose leadership became infested with dry rot, who believed in taking instead of giving . . . who didn't realize that the only assets that could not be replaced easily were the human ones." People respect a leader who keeps their interests in mind. If your focus is on what you can put into people rather than what you can get out of them, they'll love and respect you— and these create a great foundation for building relationships.

John C. Maxwell, *The 21 Indispensable Qualities of a Leader*

❖ ❖ ❖

How do you create a climate where the truth is heard? We offer four basic practices; 1. Lead with questions, not answers. 2. Engage in dialogue and debate, not coercion. 3. Conduct autopsies, without blame. 4. *Build "red flag" mechanisms.*

Jim Collins, *Good To Great*

❖ ❖ ❖

We've all heard the criticism, "He talks too much." When was the last time you heard someone criticized for listening too much?Norm Augustine

❖ ❖ ❖

Nothing beats personal, two-way communication for fostering cooperation and teamwork and for building an attitude of trust and understanding among employees.

Bill Packard

❖ ❖ ❖

Do I Identify, Encourage, and Leverage Talent?

If you want a certain value in business, you have to reward and punish the values and performance. The key is to surround yourself with the people who have the values and the performance you want.

Jack Welch

❖ ❖ ❖

Organization doesn't really accomplish anything. Plans don't accomplish anything, either. Theories of management don't much matter. Endeavors succeed or fail because of the people involved. Only by attracting the best people will you accomplish great deeds.

Colin Powell

❖ ❖ ❖

It is a fine thing to have ability, but the ability to discover ability in others is the true test.

Elbert Hubbard

❖ ❖ ❖

I have not failed. I've just found 10,000 ways that won't work.

Thomas Alva Edison, *Graduates are Special*

❖ ❖ ❖

They may forget what you said, but they will never forget how you make them feel.

Carol Buchner

❖ ❖ ❖

Talent is passion. Talent is a love of what you are doing. It all flows from that.

Malcolm Gladwell

❖ ❖ ❖

To know oneself and talents, one should assert oneself.

Albert Camus

❖ ❖ ❖

Come to the edge, he said, we are afraid. Come to the edge, he said.
They came. He pushed them and they flew.

Guillaume Apollinaire

❖ ❖ ❖

Leaders can accomplish little without understanding and
engaging the qualities of the heart.

Daniel Goleman

❖ ❖ ❖

In everyone's life, at some time, our inner fire goes out. It is then burst into
flames by an encounter with another human being. We should all be thankful for
those human beings who rekindle the inner spirit.

Albert Schweitzer

❖ ❖ ❖

Leadership is communicating to people their worth and potential
so clearly that they come to see it in themselves.

Stephen R. Covey

❖ ❖ ❖

Never doubt that a small group of committed people can change the world.
Indeed, it is the only thing that ever has.

Margaret Mead

❖ ❖ ❖

A leader is one who knows the way, goes the way, and shows the way.

John C. Maxwell

❖ ❖ ❖

Most leaders and employees do not know what their strengths are. When you ask
them, they look at you with a blank stare, or they respond to you in
terms of subject knowledge—which is the wrong answer.

Peter Drucker

❖ ❖ ❖

Thousands of candles can be lighted from a single candle, and the life of the
candle will not be shortened. Happiness never deceases by being shared.

Buddha

❖ ❖ ❖

It is better to light a candle than to curse the darkness.

Eleanor Roosevelt

❖ ❖ ❖

As a senior leader, one of your most essential roles is the systematic development of other leaders. The ultimate test is whether or not the leaders in your organization consistently attract, position, and develop successors who are prepared to lead better than the current leaders do.

Dave Ulrich

❖ ❖ ❖

Twenty years ago the business schools would ask, "Which comes first: employees, customers, or shareholders?" It was regarded as a conundrum; any answer would get you in trouble. Well, I said the employees come first, because if they're happy and satisfied and ennobled by what they're doing, they treat your customers better, and then the customers come back, and that's good for your shareholders.

Herbert (Herb) D. Kelleher

❖ ❖ ❖

The most successful CEOs, on balance, are those who are developed inside the company--but manage to retain an outside perspective.

Joseph Bower

❖ ❖ ❖

High potentials need a series of increasingly complex assignments that gives them a chance to manage a whole business as early as possible. If leaders in larger organizations need a decade to develop and need to take the helm with a decade of service still ahead of them, they need to be identified by the time they are 30.

Joseph Bower

❖ ❖ ❖

To foster deeply committed employees, leaders need to understand the types of people who will be productive in the organization, the types of values, the types of skills they should have, what are key attitudes towards work, and the value they provide as not all workers will want the same cultural environment and values.

Tamara Erickson and Lynda Gratton

❖ ❖ ❖

Companies—even very large ones—don't need to be all things to all people. In fact, they shouldn't try to be. Each firms work environment and values should seek to match employees values and attributes.

Tamara Erickson and Lynda Gratton

❖ ❖ ❖

The finest gift you can give anyone is encouragement. Yet, almost no one gets the encouragement they need to grow to their full potential. If everyone received the encouragement they need to grow, the genius in most everyone would blossom and the world would produce abundance beyond our wildest dreams.

Sidney Madwed, *If Ignorance Is Bliss, Why Aren't There More Happy People?*

❖ ❖ ❖

There is no such whetstone, to sharpen a good wit and encourage a will to learning, as is praise.

Roger Ascham, *If Ignorance Is Bliss, Why Aren't There More Happy People?*

❖ ❖ ❖

It has been said that men, like automobiles, go forward by a series of explosions. Enthusiasm might be said to be the explosive power of the personality. It is the fuse that connects with the train of powder. Every leader needs enthusiasm to explode his industry. Enthusiasm acts as an emotional generator to set industry in motion. It supplies the initiative, determination and persistence for the proposed accomplishment.

Sterling W. Sill, *Vital Quotations*

❖ ❖ ❖

Nothing is so contagious as enthusiasm . . .. It moves stones, it charms brutes. Enthusiasm is the genius of sincerity. And truth accomplishes no victories without it.

William H. Bulwar, Vital Quotations

❖ ❖ ❖

Enthusiasm is not contrary to reason. It is reason—on fire.

Peter Marshall, *If Ignorance Is Bliss, Why Aren't There More Happy People?*

❖ ❖ ❖

Enthusiastic admiration is the first principle of knowledge and its last.

William Blake, *The Yearbook of Love and Wisdom*

❖ ❖ ❖

It is energy—the central element of which is will—that produces the miracles of enthusiasm in all ages. Everywhere it is the mainspring of what is called force of character and the sustaining power of all great action.

Samuel Smiles, *Thoughts on Leadership*

❖ ❖ ❖

The real secret of success is enthusiasm.

Walter Chrysler, *The Portable DO IT!*

❖ ❖ ❖

One of the best things you can do for people—which also attracts them to you— is to expect the best of them. I call it putting a "10" on everyone's head. It helps others think more highly of themselves, and at the same time, it also helps you. According to Jacques Wiesel, "A survey of one hundred self-made millionaires showed only one common denominator. These highly successful men and women could only see the good in people."   Benjamin Disraeli understood and practiced this concept, and it was one of the secrets of his charisma. He once said, "The greatest good you can do for another is not just to share your riches but to reveal to him his own."
If you appreciate others, encourage them, and help them reach their potential, they will love you for it.

John C. Maxwell, *The 21 Indispensable Qualities of a Leader*

❖ ❖ ❖

One well-cultivated talent, deepened and enlarged, is worth 100 shallow faculties. The first law of success in this day, when so many things are clamoring for attention, is concentration—to bend all the energies to one point, and to go directly to that point, looking neither to the right nor to the left.

William Matthews, *Thoughts On Success*

❖ ❖ ❖

Focus 70 Percent on Strengths   Effective leaders who reach their potential spend more time focusing on what they do well than on what they do wrong. Leadership expert Peter Drucker notes, "The great mystery isn't that people do things badly but that they occasionally do a few things well. The only thing that is universal is incompetence. Strength is always specific! Nobody ever commented, for example, that the great violinist Jascha Heifetz probably couldn't play the trumpet very well." To be successful, focus on your strengths and develop them. That's where you should pour your time, energy, and resources.

John C. Maxwell, *The 21 Indispensable Qualities of a Leader*

❖ ❖ ❖

When a distinguished but elderly scientist states that something is possible he is almost certainly right. When he states that something is impossible, he is very probably wrong.

Arthur C. Clarke, *If Ignorance Is Bliss, Why Aren't There More Happy People?*

❖ ❖ ❖

The ability to set stretch goals is a critical piece of motivating people to achieve exceptional results. We found in our research that setting stretch goals was one of the 16 differentiating behaviors. Setting stretch goals is a behavior that is easy to talk about but harder to do. Some propose a simple path: develop what you think is a reasonable goal, then multiply by two. In the end, many leaders back off because they are uncomfortable asking others to take on a task that they themselves view as unreasonable or impossible. The first step in setting stretch goals is for you to believe in the stretch capacity of people.

John H. Zenger and Joseph Folkman, *The Extraordinary Leader*

❖ ❖ ❖

I can state flatly that heavier than air flying machines are impossible.

Lord Kelvin, *If Ignorance Is Bliss, Why Aren't There More Happy People?*

❖ ❖ ❖

Initiative is to success what a lighted match is to a candle.

Orlando A. Battista, *Thoughts On Success*

❖ ❖ ❖

Leaders who were rated as highly inspirational were also rated as having positive expectations of others. It appears that inspirational leaders have faith in the people with whom they work. They believe that others are capable of great accomplishments. They believe others will work hard, follow through on assignments, and do whatever is needed to accomplish goals. Having positive expectations of others predisposes leaders to expect more, check less, and encourage people to give their best. Having lofty expectations of others is closely related to inspiring them.

John H. Zenger and Joseph Folkman, *The Extraordinary Leader*

❖ ❖ ❖

When nobody around you seems to measure up, it's time to check your yardstick.

Bill Lemley, *Everyday Greatness*, by Stephen R. Covey

❖ ❖ ❖

One cool judgment is worth a thousand hasty counsels. The thing to be supplied is light, not heat.

Woodrow Wilson, *The Papers of Woodrow Wilson*

❖ ❖ ❖

An effective leader will make it a priority to help his or her people produce good results in two ways:

1} Make sure people know what their goals are, and

2) Do everything possible to support, encourage, and coach them to accomplish those goals

Your role as a leader is even more important than you might imagine. You have the power to help people become winners.

Ken Blanchard, *The Heart of a Leader*

❖ ❖ ❖

Motivation will almost always beat mere talent.

Norman R. Augustine, "Augustine's Laws", *The Manager's Book of Quotations*

❖ ❖ ❖

Remember, a dead fish can float downstream, but it takes a live one to swim upstream.

William Claude (W.C.) Fields, Mason, "Never Trust a Man Who Doesn't Drink", *The Manager's Book of Quotations*

❖ ❖ ❖

Opportunities are usually disguised as hard work, so most people don't recognize them.

Ann Landers, Rowes, "The Book of Quotes", *The Manager's Book of Quotations*

❖ ❖ ❖

People are the key to success in any undertaking, including business. The foremost distinguishing feature of effective managers seems to be their ability to recognize talent and to surround themselves with able colleagues.

Norman R. Augustine, "Augustine's Laws", *The Manager's Book of Quotations*

❖ ❖ ❖

The greatest good you can do for another is not just to share your riches but to reveal to him his own.

Benjamin Disraeli, *Everyday Greatness,* by Stephen R. Covey

❖ ❖ ❖

Mediocrity knows nothing higher than itself, but talent instantly recognizes genius.

Sherlock Holmes (Arthur Conan Doyle), "The Valley of Fear", *The Manager's Book of Quotations*

❖ ❖ ❖

One of the greatest talents of all is the talent to recognize and to develop talent in others.

Frank Tyger, *Thoughts On Success*

❖ ❖ ❖

Talent for talent's sake is a bauble and a show. Talent working with joy in the cause of universal truth lifts the possessor to a new power as a benefactor.

Ralph Waldo Emerson, *Thoughts on Leadership*

❖ ❖ ❖

Catch someone doing something right.

Kenneth Blanchard and Spencer Johnson

❖ ❖ ❖

One learns peoples through the heart, not the eyes or the intellect.

Mark Twain

❖ ❖ ❖

Hire people who are better than you are, then leave them to get on with it. Look for people who will aim for the remarkable, who will not settle for the routine.

David Ogilvy

❖ ❖ ❖

Never try to teach a pig to sing; it wastes your time and it annoys the pig.

Paul Dickson

❖ ❖ ❖

I've found that prayers work best...when you have big players.

Knute Rockne, Notre Dame Football Coach

❖ ❖ ❖

Do I Lead in Ways that Develop and Empower Others?

Knowing where to lead people is not the same as convincing them to follow you.

D.H. Everett

❖ ❖ ❖

All great leaders seek to bring out the best in the people that there are leading by delegation, teaching, gaining engagement, getting people to produce and ultimately get the job done.

Robert K. Greenleaf

❖ ❖ ❖

Leaders must help people find out and clarify what their strengths are and how to capitalize on them...few organizations have developed a systematic process for the maximization and efficient use of their human resources.

Marcus Buckingham

❖ ❖ ❖

Leadership is communicating to people their worth and potential so clearly that they come to see it in themselves.

Stephen R. Covey

❖ ❖ ❖

The most creative and productive work comes when people freely make commitments to one another, not when bosses tell them what to do.

Jim Collins, *Good to Great*

❖ ❖ ❖

A good leader inspires a team to have confidence in the leader. A great leader inspires a team to have confidence in themselves.

Richard Kovacevich

❖ ❖ ❖

Avoid having your ego so close to your position that when your position falls, your ego goes with it.

Colin Powell

❖ ❖ ❖

If you wish to make a man your enemy, tell him simply,
"You are wrong." This method works every time.

Henry C. Link

❖ ❖ ❖

The believers are like brothers to one another; so, promote peace and
reconciliation among them, and fear Allah, that you may receive mercy.

Surah 49: Ayah 10)

❖ ❖ ❖

Always recognize that human individuals are ends, and do
not use them as means to your end.

Immanuel Kant

❖ ❖ ❖

Each of us is an actor trying to impress an audience, to take the center of
the stage. But if you want to pay close attention to another human being,
you must train your own attention-hungry ego to stop striving for the
spotlight and let it fall on the other person.

Donald E. Smith, *Everyday Greatness,* by Stephen R. Covey

❖ ❖ ❖

Call upon each other, and be kind, cordial, and gracious to each other.
Be congenial in your brotherhood just as the almighty has commanded you.

BOOK OF al-usool FROM al-kaafi

❖ ❖ ❖

Grambling football coach Eddie Robinson cared for every individual on his team.
When they built a new stadium they placed a huge marker at the
entrance: Robinson: "Where Everybody Is Somebody."

Jerome Brondfield, *Eddie Robinson's Game Plan for Life*

❖ ❖ ❖

As ye would that men should do to you, do ye also to them likewise

Luke 6:31

❖ ❖ ❖

The more effective diversity training courses set a new, organization wide, explicit ground rule that makes bias in any form out-of-bounds, and so encourages
people who have been silent witnesses and bystanders to voice their discomforts and objections. Another active ingredient in diversity courses is perspective-taking, a stance that encourages empathy and tolerance.
To the degree that people come to understand the pain of those who feel discriminated against, they are more likely to speak out against it.

Daniel Goleman, *Emotional Intelligence*

❖ ❖ ❖

If you neglect any one of the four parts of the whole person, you turn a person into a thing. A thing lacks motivation. You will have to control and manage this employee to motivate him or her. Effectively managing an employee requires that you treat him or her as a "whole person."

Stephen R. Covey

❖ ❖ ❖

If our people are our greatest asset...and words are not mere rhetoric...then should we not insist that our people maximize all their capabilities each and every
day, and that they drive for ever greater results?

Susan Wakhungu-Githuku

❖ ❖ ❖

Within every human being lies a sleeping tiger that is about 98% asleep. The role of a leader is to give their tail a twist and see what magic, what vigor, what passion, and what real energy can be released.

Collin Hall

❖ ❖ ❖

Recalling the pep talk he gave the Dallas Cowboys before their victory in the 1993 Super Bowl game: "I told them that if I laid a two-by-four across the room everybody there could walk across it and not fall, because of focus would be that we were going to walk that two-by-four. But if I put that same two-by-four ten stories high between two buildings, only a few would make it, because the focus would be on falling."

Jimmy Johnson, *Everyday Greatness,* by Stephen R. Covey

❖ ❖ ❖

How do I delegate responsibility?

Effective managers practice "Stewardship delegation" (Habit 1) rather than "gofer delegation" To practice stewardship delegation.

Focus on results, not methods. Make expectations clear, but let team members choose how to get results. (Of course, new team member may need coaching in methods.)

Ask, "These are the results we want—how do you think we should get there?"

Delegate to team members tasks that will help them build their own capabilities.

For major tasks, ask team members to write you a "manager's letter" outlining their understanding of the task and the results expected.

Follow up. Decide together how you will hold the team member accountable.

Franklin Covey, *Management Essentials*

❖ ❖ ❖

Leaders in our organization needed to have 4 E's and a P. 4E's = Energy, Energize, Edge, and Execute. All wrapped in a big P. P = Passion. How much passion do they have for the job? How much do they want the job? Do these people have the values and performance that will help your organization achieve its' mission. Performance is the ticket to the game. Values are what get people promoted.

Jack Welch

❖ ❖ ❖

Leadership begins when it stops being about you and it starts being about your team. It is found when a leader realizes that they are going to win because of the reflected glory of their team.

Jack Welch

❖ ❖ ❖

The ultimate leader is one who is willing to develop people to the point that they eventually surpass him or her in knowledge and ability.

Fred A. Manske, Jr.

❖ ❖ ❖

And when we think we lead, we are most led.

Lord Byron

❖ ❖ ❖

A leader takes people where they want to go. A great leader takes where they don't necessarily want to go but ought to be.

Rosalynn Carter

❖ ❖ ❖

The whole is greater than the sum of its parts. Value differences.

Stephen R. Covey

❖ ❖ ❖

The key to motivating superb performance from your team is to Think Win-Win. This simply means that everyone wins all of the time—manager and worker, the team and the team member, the supplier and the customer.

Stephen R. Covey

❖ ❖ ❖

We are all in the gutter, but some of us are looking at the stars.

Oscar Wilde

❖ ❖ ❖

If you have inspired someone to do more, learn more, be more, then you are a leader.

Margaret Thatcher

❖ ❖ ❖

Leadership is the greatest of all the arts and sciences because it deals with setting vision, setting direction, unleashing talent, motivating people, and delivering sustainable results.

Michael K. Simpson

❖ ❖ ❖

A leader should have some core philosophy and belief against which he can judge the important issues as they arise. Unless he has that bedrock to fall back on, the unexpected storms that blow up will toss him about like a cork. Without such a foundation, a leader may be able to survive, be he won't be a leader….

James Callaghan, former British Prime Minister

❖ ❖ ❖

Most leaders don't need to learn what to do. They need to learn what not to do.

Peter Drucker

❖ ❖ ❖

Effective leadership requires the achievement of business results in the right way — without demeaning, demoralizing, or destroying people.

Michael Feiner, *The Feiner Points of Leadership*

❖ ❖ ❖

Nobody knows what is the best he can do.

Arturo Toscanini, "Wisdom of Sarnoff and the World of RCA",
The Manager's Book of Quotations

❖ ❖ ❖

May I share with you one of the principles that governs my life? It is the realization that what I receive I must pass on to others. The knowledge that I have
acquired must not remain imprisoned in my brain. I owe it to many men and women to do something with it. I feel the need to pay back what was given to me. Call it gratitude. Isn't this what education is all about?

Elie Wiesel

❖ ❖ ❖

Genius is initiative on fire.

Holbrook Jackson, "Platitudes in the Making", *The Manager's Book of Quotations*

❖ ❖ ❖

Any kind of knowledge gives a certain amount of power. A knowledge of details has served in many a crisis. A knowledge of details has often caught an error before it became a catastrophe.

Aimee Buchanan, *Thoughts On Leadership*

❖ ❖ ❖

I start with the premise that the function of leadership is to produce more leaders, not more followers.

Ralph Nader, *Time*, November 8, 1976, *The Manager's Book of Quotations*

❖ ❖ ❖

The way to get people to build a ship is not to teach them carpentry, assign them tasks and give them schedules to meet; but to inspire them to long for the infinite immensity of the sea.

Antoine de Saint-Exupéry, *If Ignorance Is Bliss, Why Aren't There More Happy People?*

❖ ❖ ❖

A leader takes people where they want to go. A great leader takes people where they don't necessarily want to go, but ought to be.

Rosalynn Carter, *Everyday Greatness,* by Stephen R. Covey

❖ ❖ ❖

To be a leader is far more than just to be a good man. Leadership is the ability to make goodness operate in the lives of others.

Sterling W. Sill, *Vital Quotations*

❖ ❖ ❖

It's a funny thing about life; if you refuse to accept anything but the best, you very often get it

W. Somerset Maugham, *Age Doesn't Matter Unless You're a Cheese.*

❖ ❖ ❖

When love and skill work together, expect a masterpiece.

John Ruskin, *The Portable DO IT!*

❖ ❖ ❖

How can I effectively motivate the team?   Effective managers help people become motivated by ensuring that they involve the "whole person"—the body, the heart, the mind, and the spirit—in the work. Make sure you know the answers to these questions for each team member:

Body: Are you healthy? Are you keeping fit? Are you compensated fairly?

Heart: What do you love doing? What job–related opportunities are you passionate about?

Mind: What are you really good at? What opportunities do you see here for personal growth?

Spirit: What contribution do you want to make here?

Management Essentials

❖ ❖ ❖

True success is the only thing that you cannot have unless and until you have offered it to others.

Sri Chinmoy, *Thoughts On Success*

❖ ❖ ❖

I cannot do what most of my employees can do, and I'm pleased to let them know it by showing respect for the jobs they do. If I do know how to do their job, I keep that to myself. I want them to feel I'm dependent on them.

Judith Ann Eigen, Speech, New York City, January 4, 1988, *The Manager's Book of Quotations*

❖ ❖ ❖

A severely impaired person never knows his hidden strength until he is treated like a normal human being and encouraged to try to shape his own life. Annie Sullivan regarded the blind as human beings endowed with rights to education, recreation, and employment, ad she strove to arrange my life accordingly Teacher believed in me and I resolved not to betray her faith.

Helen Keller

❖ ❖ ❖

If you have an apple and I have an apple and we exchange these apples then you and I will still each have one apple. But if you have an idea and I have an idea and we exchange these ideas, then each of us will have two ideas.

George Bernard Shaw, *If Ignorance Is Bliss, Why Aren't There More Happy People?*

❖ ❖ ❖

Nothing creates more self-respect among employees than being included in the process of making decisions.

Judith M. Bardwick, "The Plateauing Trap", *The Manager's Book of Quotations*

❖ ❖ ❖

When you find a man who knows his job and is willing to take responsibility, keep out of his way and don't bother him with unnecessary supervision. What you may think is cooperation is nothing by interference.

Thomas Dreier, *Thoughts On Leadership*

❖ ❖ ❖

The art of choosing men is not nearly so difficult as the art of enabling those one has chosen to attain their full worth.

Napoleon Bonaparte

❖ ❖ ❖

Dictators ride to and fro upon tigers which they dare not dismount. And the tigers are getting hungry.

Winston Churchill

❖ ❖ ❖

Leadership is not magnetic personality, that can just as well be a glib tongue. It is not "making friends and influencing people", that is flattery. Leadership is lifting a person's vision to higher sights, the raising of a person's performance to a higher standard, the building of a personality beyond its normal limitations.

Peter F. Drucker

❖ ❖ ❖

Before you are a leader, success is all about growing yourself. When you become a leader, success is all about growing others.

Jack Welch

❖ ❖ ❖

The function of leadership is to produce more leaders, not more followers.

Ralph Nader

❖ ❖ ❖

How do you know you have won? When the energy is coming the other way and when your people are visibly growing individually and as a group.

Sir John Harvey-Jones

❖ ❖ ❖

The vision is really about empowering workers, giving them all the information about what's going on so they can do a lot more than they've done in the past.

Bill Gates

❖ ❖ ❖

If people know you care, it brings out the best in them.

Richard Branson

❖ ❖ ❖

Do I Encourage Creative Methods and Collaborative Solutions?

When in doubt, make a fool of yourself. There is a microscopically thin line between being brilliantly creative and acting like the most gigantic idiot on earth. So what the hell, leap.

Cynthia Heimel

❖ ❖ ❖

The creative person wants to be a know-it-all. He wants to know about all kinds of things: ancient history, nineteenth century mathematics, current manufacturing techniques, flower arranging and hog futures. Because he never knows when these ideas might come together to form a new idea. It may happen six minutes later or six months or six years down the road. But he has faith that it will happen.

Carl Ally, *A Whack on the Side of the Head*

❖ ❖ ❖

Creativity represents a miraculous coming together of the uninhibited energy of a child with its apparent opposite and enemy, the sense of order imposed on the disciplined adult intelligence.

Norman Podhoretz

❖ ❖ ❖

Few ideas are in themselves practical. It is for want of imagination in applying them, rather than in acquiring them that they fail. The creative process does not end with an idea—it only starts with an idea.

John Arnold

❖ ❖ ❖

Most managers are rewarded if their unit operates efficiently and effectively. A highly creative unit, in contrast, might appear ineffective and uneven, and rather crazy to an outside or inside observer.

William G. Dyer, *Strategies for Managing Change*

❖ ❖ ❖

Creativity and imagination can solve almost any problem. The creative act, the defeat of a habit by originality, overcomes everything.

George Lois

❖ ❖ ❖

Never tell people how to do things. Tell them what to do and they will surprise you with their ingenuity.

George S. Patton

❖ ❖ ❖

Every great advance in natural knowledge has involved the absolute rejection of authority.

Thomas Huxley

❖ ❖ ❖

Creativity represents a miraculous coming together of the uninhibited energy of the child with its apparent opposite and enemy, the sense of order imposed on the disciplined adult intelligence.

Norman Podhoretz

❖ ❖ ❖

Elizabeth Barrett Browning once said, "Light tomorrow with today!" That is great advice, and following it means we have to get fired up *today*, aflame with the desire to follow our dreams.

To fan the flames, we need to be enthusiastically supportive of our ideas, no matter how crazy or farfetched they seem. We are *all* creative—we have only to tune in to our night dreams to verify that—but so many of us throw the cold water of "I can't do that" or "My ideas aren't *really* very good" onto our original notions. Dampened by doubt, the fires of creativity can fizzle. It's up to us to fan the flames of our own creativity. Believing in ourselves is the most powerful bellows we can use to kindle the fire of creative thought.

Sue Patton Thoele, Woman's Book of Soul

❖ ❖ ❖

Nothing stops an organization faster than people who believe that the way you worked yesterday is the best way to work tomorrow.

Jon Madonna

❖ ❖ ❖

Creativity is more than just being different. Anybody can play weird; that's easy. What's hard is to be as simple as Bach. Making the simple complicated is commonplace; making the complicated simple, awesomely simple—that's creativity.

Charles Mingus

❖ ❖ ❖

Creativity is allowing yourself to make mistakes.
Art is knowing which ones to keep.

Scott Adams

❖ ❖ ❖

If at first you don't succeed, try, try again. Then give up.
There's no use in being a damn fool about it.

W.C. Fields

❖ ❖ ❖

The key to every man is his thought . . . . He can only be reformed by showing him a new idea which commands his own.

Ralph Waldo Emerson, "Circle," *Essays: First Series*

❖ ❖ ❖

Ideas are like rabbits. You get a couple and learn how to handle them, and pretty soon you have a dozen of them.

John Steinbeck, *If Ignorance Is Bliss, Why Aren't There More Happy People?*

❖ ❖ ❖

"Almost nothing new works" is a common expression among innovative persons. This phrase is not spoken, however, in a defeatist tone of voice, but rather in simple recognition of the fact that innovation is a high risk venture.

Lyle E. Schaller, "The Change Agent", *The Manager's Book of Quotations*

❖ ❖ ❖

Legend has it that Elias Howe intently studied his mother sewing, then invented the sewing machine.... Howe did not try to duplicate with his invention precisely what his mother did. He merely tried to duplicate the result.

Daniel E. Whitney, *Harvard Business Review,* May/June 1986,
The Manager's Book of Quotations

❖ ❖ ❖

It is precisely because the unexpected jolts us out of our preconceived notions, our assumptions, our certainties, that it is such a fertile source of innovation. In no other area are innovative opportunities less risky and their pursuit less arduous. Yet the unexpected success is almost totally neglected; worse, managements tend actively to reject it.

Peter F. Drucker, "Innovation and Entrepreneurship", *The Daily Drucker*

❖ ❖ ❖

Often a dash of judgment is better than a flash of genius.

Howard W. Newton, Thoughts on Leadership

❖ ❖ ❖

We can be knowledgeable with other men's knowledge but we cannot be wise with other men's wisdom.

Michel de Montaigne, *If Ignorance Is Bliss, Why Aren't There More Happy People?*

❖ ❖ ❖

The new leader is a facilitator, not an order giver.

John Naisbitt, "Megatrends", *The Manager's Book of Quotations*

❖ ❖ ❖

From error to error; one discovers the entire truth.

Sigmund Freud, *The Portable DO IT!*

❖ ❖ ❖

The effects of opposition are wonderful. There are men who rise refreshed on hearing a threat—men to whom a crisis which intimidates and paralyzes the majority comes graceful and beloved as a bride!

Ralph Waldo Emerson, *Thoughts on Leadership*

❖ ❖ ❖

You've got to have an atmosphere where people can make mistakes. If we're not making mistake we're not going anywhere.

Gordon Forward, "Thriving on Chaos", *The Manager's Book of Quotations*

❖ ❖ ❖

Originality is unexplored territory. You get there by carrying a canoe. You can't take a taxi.

Alan Alda, *If Ignorance Is Bliss, Why Aren't There More Happy People?*

❖ ❖ ❖

Do I Manage People and Processes Effectively?

Effective leadership is putting first things first. Effective management is discipline, carrying it out.

Stephen R. Covey

❖ ❖ ❖

The key to being a good manager is keeping the people who hate me away from those who are still undecided.

Casey Stengel

❖ ❖ ❖

The conventional definition of management is getting work done through people, but real management is developing people through work.

Agha Hasan Abedi

❖ ❖ ❖

Every team has a unique function it performs. Your **core work process** is the way you carry out that work. You know you have a great core work process when it: (1) is aligned to achieve your highest priorities, (2) creates unquestionable value for customers/stakeholders, (3) enables people to give their best, (4) operates independently of the leader, and (5) endures beyond the leader.

FtanklinCovey's Leadership Greatness work session:
Great leaders, great teams, and great results.

❖ ❖ ❖

If you pick the right people and give them the opportunity to spread their wings—and put compensation as a carrier behind it—you almost don't have to manage them.

Jack Welch

❖ ❖ ❖

Good management is the art of making problems so interesting and their solutions so constructive that everyone wants to get to work and deal with them.

Paul Hawken

❖ ❖ ❖

Groups become teams through *disciplined action.* They *shape* a common purpose, *agree* on performance goals, *define* a common working approach, *develop* high levels of complementary skills, and *hold* themselves mutually responsible for results. And, as with any effective discipline, they never stop doing any of these things.

Jon R. Katzenbach and Douglas K. Smith, "The Wisdom of Teams",
Harper Business, 1993

❖ ❖ ❖

Any organization develops people; it has no choice. It either helps them grow or it stunts them. What do we know about developing people? Quite a bit. We certainly know what not to do, and those don'ts are easier to spell out than the dos. First, one does not try to build upon people's weakness. One can expect adults to develop manners and behavior and to learn skills and knowledge. But one has to use people's personalities the way they are, not the way we would like them to be. A second don't is to take a narrow and shortsighted view of the development of people.

In developing people the lesson is to focus on strengths. Then make really stringent demands, and take the time and trouble (it's hard work) to review performance. Sit down with people and say: "This is what you and I committed ourselves to a year ago. How have you done? What have you done well?"

Peter F. Drucker, *Managing the Non-Profit Organization*

❖ ❖ ❖

"Management" means, in the last analysis, the substitution of thought for brawn and muscle, of knowledge for folkways and superstition, and of cooperation for force. It means the substitution of responsibility for obedience to rank, and of authority of performance for authority of rank.

Peter F. Drucker, "People and Performance", *The Manager's Book of Quotations*

❖ ❖ ❖

Because a thing seems difficult for you, do not think it
impossible for anyone to accomplish.

Marcus Aurelius

❖ ❖ ❖

For a person who cherishes compassion and love, the practice of tolerance is essential; and for that, an enemy is indispensable.

The Dalai Lama

❖ ❖ ❖

Management creates economic and social development. Economic and social development is the result of management. It can be said, without too much oversimplification, that there are no "underdeveloped countries." There are only "undermanaged" ones. Japan a hundred and forty years ago was an underdeveloped country by every material measurement. But it very quickly produced management of great competence, indeed, of excellence. This means that management is the prime mover and that development is a consequence. Development, in other words, is a matter of human energies rather than of economic wealth. And the generation and direction of human energies is the task of management.

Peter F. Drucker, "The Ecological Vision", *The Daily Drucker*

❖ ❖ ❖

Management always lives, works, and practices in and for an institution, which is a human community held together by a bond: the work bond. And precisely because the object of management is a human community held together by the work bond for a common purpose, management always deals with the nature of Man and (as all of us with any practical experience have learned) with Good and Evil, as well. I have learned more theology as a practicing management consultant than when I taught religion.

Peter F. Drucker, "Teaching the Work of Management,"
New Management, The Daily Drucker

❖ ❖ ❖

No part of the productive resources of industry operates at a lower efficiency than the human resources. The few enterprises that have been able to tap this unused reservoir of human ability and attitude have achieved spectacular increases in productivity and output. In the better use of human resources lies the major opportunity for increasing productivity in the great majority of enterprises—so that the management of people should be the first and foremost concern of operating managements, rather than the management of things and techniques, on which attention has been focused so far.
We also know what makes for the efficiency and productivity of the human resources of production. It is not primarily skill or pay; it is, first and foremost, an attitude—the one we call the "managerial attitude." By this we mean an attitude that makes the individual see his job, his work, and his product the way a manager sees them, that is, in relation to the group and the product as a whole.

Peter F. Drucker, "The New Society", *The Daily Drucker*

❖ ❖ ❖

Do I Give Respectful, Honest, and Useful Feedback?

Transparency and candor are fundamental to all performance evaluations. Management owes to their people to let them know exactly where they stand.

Jack Welch

❖ ❖ ❖

The key to developing people is to catch them doing something right.

Ken Blanchard and Spencer Johnson, *The One Minute Manager*

❖ ❖ ❖

High performers:

Are genuinely concerned about the development of others' careers

Give individuals an appropriate balance of positive and corrective performance feedback

Give honest feedback

Take interest in the work of others

Support others' growth and success

Poor performers:

Wait too long to give others feedback

Try to keep good people rather than allowing them to take on developmental opportunities

John H. Zenger and Joseph Folkman, *The Extraordinary Leader*

❖ ❖ ❖

I firmly believe that providing feedback is the most cost-effective strategy for improving performance and instilling satisfaction. It can be done quickly, it costs nothing, and it can turn people around fast.

Ken Blanchard, *The Heart of a Leader*

❖ ❖ ❖

All the strategic planning, financial rejiggering and number crunching in the world won't help if it can't succeed in changing human behavior. And that it seems, is the hardest thing of all to do.

Sarah Bartlett, *Business Week*, August 24, 1987, *The Manager's Book of Quotations*

❖ ❖ ❖

In its original sense in systems theory, *feedback* meant the exchange of data about how one part of a system in working, with the understanding that one part affects all others in the system so that any part heading off course could be changed for the better. In a company everyone is part of the system, and so feedback is the lifeblood of the organization—the exchange of information that lets people now if the job they are doing is going well or needs to be fine-tuned, upgraded, or redirected entirely. Without feedback people are in the dark, they have no idea how they stand with their boss, with their peers, or in terms of what is expected of them, and any problems will only get worse as times passes.

Daniel Goleman, *Emotional Intelligence*

❖ ❖ ❖

An artful critique can be one of the most helpful messages a manager can send. An artful critique focuses on what a person has done and can do rather than reading a mark of character into a job poorly done. As Larson Observes, "A character attack—calling someone stupid or incompetent—misses the point. You immediately put him on the defensive, so that he's no longer receptive to what you have to tell him about how to do things better." That advice, of course, is precisely the same as for married couples airing their grievances.

Daniel Goleman, *Emotional Intelligence*

❖ ❖ ❖

I *choose* to feel good about myself. That way I am more open to learning. If people give me negative feedback or criticize something I do. I don't interpret what they are saying as meaning that I am a "bad" person. The belief that I control my own self-esteem permits me to listen to and hear their feedback in a nondefensive way—looking to see if there is something I can learn.

Ken Blanchard, *The Heart of a Leader*

❖ ❖ ❖

In the past we have often focused our efforts on patching over weaknesses. When executives are given a 360-degree feedback report, the consistent reaction is to ignore the pages describing their strengths, and immediately focus on weaknesses, which in most cases are simply behaviors that are rated as less positive rather than real fatal flaws. It is as if strengths are givens, and the thing to work on is weaknesses or less positive areas. Increasingly we are convinced this is a mistake. It is far better to magnify strengths, or create strengths out of those characteristics that are in positive territory but not fully developed. Leaders who are moderately effective and preoccupy themselves with incremental improvement of less positive issues will never move from good to great.

John H. Zenger and Joseph Folkman, *The Extraordinary Leader*

❖ ❖ ❖

"I think every human being, Arthur Levitt (head of SEC) or the janitor or the waitress or the doctor or the professor, needs and craves validation and positive feedback." And the big misconception is to think that it has to be money. "It can be really small things," said Whitman, "telling someone, 'You did a really great job, you were recognized as doing a great history paper.' Our users say to us [about eBay's star system], Where else can you wake up in the morning and see how much people like you?"

Meg Whitman, *The World Is Flat*

❖ ❖ ❖

There are three responses people can receive from leadership concerning their performance—positive, negative, or no response at all. Only one response of the three tends to increase good performance—the positive one. And yet, the major leadership style used today is "leave alone—zap!".... Many leaders notice their people doing things right and think well of them. Unfortunately, the do not always put those positive thoughts into words. As a result, this good performance gets no response. If you want to get and maintain good performance, you must let your people know you notice and care about the things they do right. Share your good thoughts.

Ken Blanchard, *The Heart of a Leader*

❖ ❖ ❖

There is nothing that so kills the ambitions of a man as criticism from his superiors. So I am anxious to praise but loath to find fault. I have yet to find the man,
however exalted his station, who did not do better work and put forth greater effort under a spirit of approval than under a spirit of criticism.

Charles Schwab, *How to Win Friends and Influence People*, by Dale Carnegie

❖ ❖ ❖

Many well-intentioned leaders wait to praise their people until they do things exactly right—complete the project or accomplish the goal. The problem here is that they could wait forever. You see "exactly right" behavior is made up of a whole series of approximately right behaviors. It makes more sense to praise progress—it's a moving target.   Can you imagine standing a child up and saying, "Walk," and when he falls down, you say, "I told you to walk!" and then spank him. Of course not. You stand the child up and he wobbles a bit. You shout, "You stood!" and shower him with hugs and kisses. The next day, he wobbles a step and you are all over him with praise. Gradually, the child gains confidence until he finally walks. It's the same with adults. Catch them doing things right—and in the beginning, approximately right is fine.

Ken Blanchard, *The Heart of a Leader*

❖ ❖ ❖

A pat on the back though only a few vertebrae removed from a kick
in the pants, is miles ahead in results.

Bennett Cerf, *Everyday Greatness*, by Stephen R. Covey

❖ ❖ ❖

I can live for two months on a good compliment.

Mark Twain, *Everyday Greatness*, by Stephen R. Covey

❖ ❖ ❖

If one by one we counted people out for the least fault it wouldn't take
us long to get so we had no one left to live with.

Robert Frost

❖ ❖ ❖

Nothing is easier than fault finding; no talent, no self-denial,
no brains are required to set up in the grumbling business.

Robert West

❖ ❖ ❖

Leaders need to be more candid with those they purport to lead. Sharing good
news is easy. When it comes to the more troublesome negative news, be candid
and take responsibility. Don't withhold unpleasant possibilities and don't pass off
bad news to subordinates to deliver. Level with employees about problems in a
timely fashion.

Jon Huntsman

❖ ❖ ❖

We strive to tell everyone everything we can. We want a culture with open
dialogue and straight answers. In terms of our work with employees, we have
been direct with them even when they don't like the answer. Our goal is not to
please everyone but instead for them to trust that what we tell them is the truth.
You can't work the tough issues we face unless everyone, starting with the senior
team, trusts one another.

Greg Brenneman

❖ ❖ ❖

How Do I Effectively Use Power and Influence?

Leadership is about successfully using your power, your privileges',
and your influence to bless others.

Dr. Blaine Lee

❖ ❖ ❖

Power can be seen as power *with* rather than power *over*, and it can be used for
competence and cooperation, rather than dominance and control.

Anne L. Barstow

❖ ❖ ❖

Outstanding leaders go out of the way to boost the self-esteem of their personnel.
If people believe in themselves, it's amazing what they can accomplish.

Sam Walton

❖ ❖ ❖

When you stop using your discretionary effort, you stop looking at
creative things you can do. If you want people coming to work with
only half their brains, put them under stress.

Richard Boyatzis

❖ ❖ ❖

Greatness lies not in being strong, but in the right use of strength.

Henry Ward Beecher

❖ ❖ ❖

To make no mistakes is not in the power of man or women; but from
their errors and mistakes the wise and good learn wisdom for the future.

Plutarch

❖ ❖ ❖

The art of being wise is knowing what to overlook.

William James

❖ ❖ ❖

It's not what people do to us that hurts us. It is our chosen response
to what they do to us that hurts us.

Stephen R. Covey

❖ ❖ ❖

The closest to disbelief a person can be is when he conceals the error of his brother
in faith intending to dishonor him and use it against him.

imam ja'far al-saadiq, book of al-usool from al-kaafi, Vol. 2

❖ ❖ ❖

Being outside the mainstream allows for a certain detachment from the
conventional wisdom and prevents managers from being cowed by a powerful
CEO.

Joseph Bower

❖ ❖ ❖

So often we thing of a leader who is hard charging, aggressive, forceful, take-no-
prisoners type… A servant leader is one who encourages, collaborates, trusts,
listens, has foresight, and possesses the ethical use of power and empowerment
with others.

Robert K. Greenleaf

❖ ❖ ❖

Throughout human history, our greatest leaders and thinkers have used the
power of words to transform our emotions, to enlist us in their causes, and to
shape the course of destiny. Words can create not only emotions, they create
actions. And from our actions flow the results of our lives.

Tony Robbins

❖ ❖ ❖

A great man shows his greatness by the way he treats little men.

Thomas Carlyle

❖ ❖ ❖

The responsibility of leadership is one of shaping our own and
others' lives, hopefully for the better.

Delorese Ambrose

❖ ❖ ❖

There is only one thing that will really train the human mind and that is the voluntary use of the mind by the man himself. You may aid him, you may guide him, you may suggest to him, and, above all else, you may inspire him. But the only thing worth having is that which he gets by his own exertions, and what he gets is in direct proportion to what he puts into it.

Albert L. Lowell, *Thoughts on Leadership*

❖ ❖ ❖

Arguments are to be avoided; they are always vulgar and often convincing.

Oscar Wilde, "The Toastmaster's Treasure Chest", *The Manager's Book of Quotations*

❖ ❖ ❖

The superior leader gets things done with very little motion. He imparts instruction not through many words but through a few deeds. He keeps informed about everything but interferes hardly at all. He is a catalyst, and though things would not get done as well if he weren't there, when they succeed he takes no credit. And because he takes no credit, credit never leaves him.

Lao-Tzu, "Tao Te Ching", *The Manager's Book of Quotations*

❖ ❖ ❖

Hundreds of studies have been conducted in the United States into how the exercise of power affects leadership…. The consistent picture of the effective leader is one who adopts the style of a "superfollower," who serves with his followers' blessing and consent, and who is able to inspire because he is first able to respond to their needs and concerns. Power, in this context, means the ability to get things done, to mobilize resources, and to draw on what is necessary to accomplish goals. Power is thus more akin to "mastery" than to "domination" or "control…." People who use power best use it directly only as necessary to get the job done. They do not worry much about it as an end to itself.

Richard T. Pascale and Anthony G. Athos, "The Art of Japanese Management", *The Manager's Book of Quotations*

❖ ❖ ❖

You do not lead by hitting people over the head — that's assault, not leadership.

Dwight D. Eisenhower

❖ ❖ ❖

He who has great power should use it lightly.

Seneca

❖ ❖ ❖

Nearly all men can stand adversity, but if you want to test a man's character, give him power.

Abraham Lincoln

❖ ❖ ❖

Behold there are many are called but few are chosen. And why are they not chosen? Because their hearts are set so much upon the things of this world, and aspire to the honors of men...the powers of heaven cannot be controlled nor handled only upon the principles of righteousness...when we undertake to cover our sins, or to gratify our pride, our vain ambition, or to exercise control or dominion or compulsion upon the souls of the children of men, in any degree of unrighteousness, behold the heavens withdraw themselves and the Spirit of the Lord is grieved. We have learned by sad experience that it is the nature and disposition of almost all men, as soon as they get a little authority, as they suppose, they will immediately begin to exercise unrighteous dominion. Hence, many are called but few are chosen.

Doctrine & Covenants Section 121: 34-37; 39-40.

❖ ❖ ❖

No power or influence can or ought to be maintained by virtue...only by persuasion, by long-suffering, by gentleness and meekness, and by love unfeigned; by kindness, and pure knowledge, which shall greatly enlarge the soul without hypocrisy, and without guile...let thy bowels be full of charity towards all men...let virtue garnish thy thoughts unceasingly.

Doctrine & Covenants Section 121: 41-43, 45

❖ ❖ ❖

How Do I Avoid Pride?

Nearly all evils in the world which people list to selfishness are really a result of Pride...It is Pride that is the chief cause of misery in every nation and family since the world began...The first step is to realize that one is proud. If you think you are not conceited, it means you are very conceited indeed.

C.S. Lewis

❖ ❖ ❖

Pride goes before destruction, a haughty spirit before the fall.

Proverbs 16:18

❖ ❖ ❖

Can you imagine your boss admitting a personal failing and outlining his efforts to stop doing it? Probably not. Leaders try to maintain a positive tone to and to get credit for doing good things -- rarely do they ceasing to do bad things.

Marshall Goldsmith

❖ ❖ ❖

The six ugliest words in the English language are: 1. Selfishness. 2. Conceited. 3. Self-Centered. 4. Egotistical. 5. Haughty. 6. Arrogant. It has been said that there are seven deadly sins: 1. Pride. 2. Envy. 3. Gluttony. 4. Lust. 5. Anger. 6. Greed. 7. Sloth.

Mahatma Gandhi

❖ ❖ ❖

Pride is a haughty attitude show by people who believe, often unjustifiably, that they are better than others.

Hal Urban

❖ ❖ ❖

No country in the world is so driven by personality, has such a hunger to identify with personalities, larger than life personalities, as this one.

Peter Jennings

❖ ❖ ❖

Pride is the first sin, the source of all other sins, and the worst sin.

Thomas Aquinas

❖ ❖ ❖

We have learned by sad experiences that it is the nature and disposition of almost all men, as soon as they get a little authority, as they suppose, they will immediately begin to exercise unrighteous dominion. Hence many are called, but few are chosen. No power or influence can or ought to be maintained...only by persuasion, by long suffering, by gentleness, and meekness, and by love unfeigned. By kindness, and pure knowledge which shall greatly enlarge the soul without hypocrisy and without guile.

Doctrine & Covenants 121: 39, 41, 42.

❖ ❖ ❖

Because their hearts are set so much upon the things of this world, and aspire to the honors of men, that they do not learn this one lesson...but when we undertake to cover our sins, gratify our pride, our vain ambitions, or to exercise control or dominion or compulsion upon the souls of the children of men, in any degree of unrighteousness the spirit is grieved...

Doctrine and Covenants 121: 35, 37

❖ ❖ ❖

Many promising reconciliations have broken down because, while both parties came prepared to forgive, neither party came prepared to be forgiven.

Charles Williams, *Healing After Loss*

❖ ❖ ❖

Measured objectively, what a man can wrest from Truth by passionate striving is utterly infinitesimal. But the striving frees us from the bonds of the self and makes us comrades of those who are the best and the greatest.

Albert Einstein, *Bite-Size Einstein*

❖ ❖ ❖

Everybody is ignorant only on different subjects.

Will Rogers—Paula McSpadden Love, *The Will Rogers Book,* Respectfully Quoted

❖ ❖ ❖

A friend of mine jokes about his latest book,

Humility and How I Attained It. It reminds me of what I call the greatest addiction in the world today—the human ego.

❖ ❖ ❖

Leaders who fall victim to this addiction want to be center stage. They often are threatened by the successes of others, so they fail to develop and use people's talents or catch them doing something right. They want to be the best— "the fairest of them all."

Ken Blanchard, *The Heart of a Leader*

❖ ❖ ❖

Great men never make bad use of their superiority; they see it, and feel it, and are not less modest. The more they have, the more they know their own deficiencies.

Jean-Jacques Rousseau, *Thoughts On Leadership*

❖ ❖ ❖

It is said that it is far more difficult to hold and maintain leadership (liberty) than it is to attain it. Success is a ruthless competitor for it flatters and nourishes our weaknesses and lulls us into complacency. We bask in the sunshine of accomplishment and lose the spirit of humility which helps us visualize all the factors which have contributed to our success. We are apt to forget that we are only one of a team, that in unity there is strength and that we are strong only as long as each unit in our organization functions with precision.

Samuel Tilden, *Thoughts On Leadership*

❖ ❖ ❖

When hosting high-ranking friends, former U.S. President, Theodore Roosevelt, was fond of taking his guests on evening walks. Inevitably, he would point skyward and recite: "That is the Spiral Galaxy of Andromeda. It is as large as our Milky Way. It is one of a hundred million galaxies. It is 2,5000,000 light years away. It consists of one hundred billion suns, many larger than your own sun." Then, following a brief silence, he would grin and say, "Now, I think we are small enough. Let's go in."

Harold E. Kohn, *Thoughts Afield*

❖ ❖ ❖

It is well to remember that the entire universe, with one trifling exception, is composed of others.

John Andrew Holmes, If Ignorance Is Bliss, Why Aren't There More Happy People?

❖ ❖ ❖

The sufficiency of my merit is to know that my merit is not sufficient.

St. Augustine

❖ ❖ ❖

No matter what accomplishments you make, somebody helped you.

Althea Gibson

❖ ❖ ❖

The greatest magnifying glasses in the world are a man's own eyes
when they look upon his own person.

Alexander Pope

❖ ❖ ❖

What I call Lovol 5 leaders build enduring greatness through a paradoxical
blend of personal humility and professional will.

Jim Collins

❖ ❖ ❖

How Do I Use My Powers of
Communication and Persuasion?

Many of our communications difficulties arise because we attack problems like James Thurber's dog Jeannie, who tried to get out of a garage by digging through the concrete floor with one paw. We constantly think other people will be persuaded by our intelligent presentation of the facts or the force of our convictions—when in reality these glance off them like raindrops off a car roof. We have totally ignored the need to prepare the ground for the emotional climate which will make people listen to us, trust us and be persuaded by us.

Eli Djeddah

❖ ❖ ❖

How well we communicate is determined not by how well we
say things but by how well we are understood.

Andrew S. Grove

❖ ❖ ❖

Franklin [Delano Roosevelt] had a good way of simplifying things.
He made people feel that he had a real understanding of things and
they felt they had about the same understanding.

Eleanor Roosevelt

❖ ❖ ❖

Communication is at the heart of our lives and connects our souls with those we love and with the soul of the world. How we communicate determines whether we build bridges or create chasms within ourselves, and between ourselves, others, the environment, and God. If our communication with ourselves is a continual crucifixion, our spirits become wounded and clamp tightly shut. A closed spirit cannot commune with others, souls to soul.
Artful communication, on the other hand, connects us to ourselves and each other, bonds us together through strands of energy, actions, and words. At best, communication becomes a daily communion, in which we express the highest and deepest within us, and share the very best of ourselves, thereby calling forth the very best from others.

Sue Patton Thoele

❖ ❖ ❖

No man is wise enough to know which avenue to the brain is best. Therefore, the sensible idea is to make all avenues available for carrying the message.

David Sarnoff

❖ ❖ ❖

When thinking about how a person communicates powerfully, most people concentrate on how a message is delivered. It was interesting to learn that one of the strongest competency companions for communicating powerfully is involving others. In other words, those who were viewed as powerful communicators asked people for their input, encouraged alternative approaches and new ideas from others, and made sure that others were in agreement. Leaders rated low in their ability to communicate tended to concentrate on getting their message delivered.

John H. Zenger and Joseph Folkman, *The Extraordinary Leader*

❖ ❖ ❖

Real communication happens when we feel safe.

Ken Blanchard

❖ ❖ ❖

Communication is the deep exchange of experience that brings the two parties to a full understanding of each other, including the understanding that they understand each other. People actually go out of their way to not communicate with people with whom they feel out of harmony.

Kenneth and Linda Schatz

❖ ❖ ❖

We cannot ignore tone of voice or attitudes. These may be just as important as the words used.

Maurice S. Trotter

❖ ❖ ❖

Be sure, when you think you are being extremely tactful, that you are not in reality running away from something you ought to face.

Frank Medlicott

❖ ❖ ❖

Handle people with gloves, but issues, barefisted.

Dagobert D. Runes

❖ ❖ ❖

Nothing astonishes men so much as commonsense and plain dealings.

Ralph Waldo Emerson

❖ ❖ ❖

Words are what hold society together; without
them we should not be human beings.

Stuart Chase

❖ ❖ ❖

I believe that words...go into the body, as effect. So they cause us to be well and
hopeful and full of high energy -- that is wondrous, funny, and cheerful.
Or, they can cause us to be depressed. They get into the body and
cause us to be sullen, sour, depressed, and finally sick.

Maya Angelou

❖ ❖ ❖

From the fruit of his lips a man is filled with good things as surely
as the work of his hands rewards him.

Proverbs 12:14

❖ ❖ ❖

Reckless words pierce like a sword, but the tongue of the wise brings healing.

Proverbs 12:18

❖ ❖ ❖

A fool gets into constant fights. His mouth is his undoing! His words endanger
him.

Proverbs 18:6-7

❖ ❖ ❖

He who guards his lips guards his life, but he who speaks rashly will come to ruin.

Proverbs 13:3

❖ ❖ ❖

Not he is great who can alter matter, but he who can alter my state of mind.

Ralph Waldo Emerson, *Nature, Addresses and Lectures*

❖ ❖ ❖

There is a great man who makes every man feel small. But the really great man is the man who makes every man feel great.

Chinese Proverb, *Thoughts On Leadership*

❖ ❖ ❖

The void created by the failure to communicate is soon
filled with poison,
drivel and misrepresentation.

C. Northcote Parkinson

❖ ❖ ❖

Developing excellent communication skills is absolutely essential to effective leadership. The leader must be able to share knowledge and ideas to transmit a sense of urgency and enthusiasm to others. If a leader can't get a message across clearly and motivate others to act on it, then having a message doesn't even matter.

Gilbert Amelio

❖ ❖ ❖

Do I Build and Celebrate the Team?

The secret of joy in work is contained in one word – excellence.
To know how to do something well is to enjoy it.

Pearl S. Buck

❖ ❖ ❖

Individual commitment to a group effort--that's what makes a team
work, a company work, , a society work, a civilization work.

Vince Lombardi

❖ ❖ ❖

Winning the Daytona 500 race is not about the car, but it's about the team..

Anonymous

❖ ❖ ❖

One of the greatest ways to engage employee performance at work
is to treat their job a little like a game. Everyone likes to feel a sense of
accomplishment and see how they are winning.

Chris McChesney

❖ ❖ ❖

Give the other person a good reputation to live up to. We do that
when we seek to catch people doing things right.

Dale Carnegie

❖ ❖ ❖

We increase whatever we praise. The whole creation responds to praise, and is
glad.

Charles Fillmore

❖ ❖ ❖

Flatter me, and I may not believe you. Criticize me, and I may not like you. Ignore
me, and I may not forgive you. Encourage me, and I may not forget you.

William Arthur Ward

❖ ❖ ❖

A cheerful look brings joy to the heart, and good news gives health to the bones.

Proverbs 15:30

❖ ❖ ❖

Few things in the world are more powerful than a positive push. A smile. A word of optimism and hope. A "you can do it" when things are tough.

Richard DeVos

❖ ❖ ❖

Give encouragement to each other, and keep strengthening one another.

Thessalonians 5:11

❖ ❖ ❖

Do not withhold good from those who deserve it, when it is in your power to act.

Proverbs 3:27

❖ ❖ ❖

The toughest thing about being a success is that you have to keep on being a success.

Irving Berlin

❖ ❖ ❖

The ability to form friendships, to make people believe in you and trust you, is one of the few absolutely fundamental qualities of success. Selling, buying, negotiating are so much smoother and easier when the parties enjoy each other's confidence. The young man who can make friends quickly will find that he will glide instead of stumbling through life.

John J. McGuirk, *Thoughts On Success*

❖ ❖ ❖

What defines great leadership? What does great leadership entail? It has many dimensions, of course. The mission of leadership, it seems to me, is to guide and enable purposeful growth of individuals and institutions . . . Purposeful growth also creates a sense of pride and excitement for employees because they are part of a winning team—and it is no wonder that is what attracts the best talent.

John E. Pepper, *Business with Integrity*

❖ ❖ ❖

If anything goes bad, I did it.
If anything goes semi-good , then we did it.

If anything goes real good, then you did it.

That's all it takes to get people to win football games.

Paul "Bear" Bryant, "Bits & Pieces 1", 1987, *The Manager's Book of Quotations*

❖ ❖ ❖

It is amazing how much people get done if they do
not worry about who gets the credit.

Swahili proverb

❖ ❖ ❖

The ratio of We's to I's is the best indicator of the development of a team.

Lewis B. Ergen

❖ ❖ ❖

The leaders who work most effectively, it seems to me, never say 'I.' And that's
not because they have trained themselves not to say 'I.' They don't think 'I.' They
think 'we'; they think 'team.' They understand their job to be to make the team
function. They accept responsibility and don't sidestep it, but 'we' gets the
credit.... This is what creates trust, what enables you to get the task done.

Peter Drucker

❖ ❖ ❖

Build for your team a feeling of oneness, of dependence on one
another and of strength to be derived by unity.

Vince Lombardi

❖ ❖ ❖

Challenge yourself each and every day to make business better. Ask: What did
we do today to make your business better? Did we gain greater focus, clarity,
engagement, and improve our ability to inspire others? Ask: Does our business
create more opportunity for others? Become an opportunity creating machine to
advance others goals, dreams, and success.

Doug DeVos

❖ ❖ ❖

What are the biggest risks to the business?

Getting too complacent. Being satisfied with our success.
We think we know it all. Not getting better

To stop being curious and not seeking for ways in how to get better.

Doug DeVos

❖ ❖ ❖

What makes you the most proud in the business?

We put our faith, hope, and dreams in our people. Seeing the people changing
their quality of lives and have success in my greatest joy.

It's all about the people you meet along the way. Know their families, kids,
accomplishments, and challenges -- stay connected to the people.

Living and promoting our values of freedom, faith, family, and rewards.

Use the golden rule and love your neighbors, "do unto others as you would have
them do unto you."

Value the differences in your business partners and leverage their skills,
capabilities, experiences and talents.

Doug DeVos

❖ ❖ ❖

What is your greatest opportunity for success in your business?

Our greatest opportunities are all around us. Build your
business around your core strengths.

Look for big needs in the business and focus on the small shifts, new ways of
aligning to those needs and opportunities (there are big and small opportunities
everywhere)

Success is about keeping it simple; We sell products and help others do the same.
Know the fundamentals of the business and execute those –
keep your focus narrow to the top 3-5 things.

Doug DeVos

❖ ❖ ❖

A group becomes a team when each member is sure enough of
himself and his contribution to praise the skill of the others.

Norman S Hidle

❖ ❖ ❖

What we need to do is learn to work in the system, by which I mean that everybody, every team, every platform, every division, every component is there not for individual competitive profit or recognition, but for contribution to the system as a whole on a win-win basis.

W. Edward Deming

❖ ❖ ❖

The way you see them is the way you treat them and the way you treat them is the way they often become.

Zig Ziglar

❖ ❖ ❖

The first responsibility of a leader is to define reality. The last is to say thank you. In between, the leader is a servant.

Max DePree

❖ ❖ ❖

Team Humor

By working faithfully eight hours a day, you may get to
be a boss and work twelve hours a day.

Robert Frost

❖ ❖ ❖

Those who think they know everything are very annoying to those of us who do.

Terry Marchal

❖ ❖ ❖

My opinions may have changed, but not the fact that I am right.

Ashleigh Brilliant

❖ ❖ ❖

Ya gots to work with what you gots to work with.

Stevie Wonder

❖ ❖ ❖

It's not that I'm lazy; it's that I just don't care.

The *Office*

❖ ❖ ❖

Life is too short to be taken too seriously and not to enjoy your
life and your career – you need to enjoy the ride.

Doug DeVos

❖ ❖ ❖

So, where's the Cannes Film Festival being held this year?

Christina Aguilera

❖ ❖ ❖

A perfect method of adding drama to life is to wait until the deadline looms large.

Alyce P. Cornyn-Selby

❖ ❖ ❖

After I hit a home run I had a habit of running the bases with my head down. I figured the pitcher already felt bad enough without me showing him up rounding the bases.

Mickey Mantle

❖ ❖ ❖

As the poet said, "Only God can make a tree"—probably because it's so hard to figure out how to get the bark on.

Woody Allen

❖ ❖ ❖

I like work; it fascinates me. I can sit and look at it for hours.

Jerome K. Jerome

❖ ❖ ❖

Tolerance is a great trait to contain, but so is the ability to shut up.

Author Unknown

❖ ❖ ❖

Never pick a fight with an ugly person—they've got nothing to lose.

Robin Williams

❖ ❖ ❖

It is good sportsmanship to not pick up lost golf balls while they are still rolling.

Author Unknown

❖ ❖ ❖

A committee is a group of people who individually can do nothing, but together can decide that nothing can be done.

Fred Allen

❖ ❖ ❖

I have never been able to understand why it is that just because I am unintelligible, nobody understands me.

Milton Mayer, *Management Essentials*

❖ ❖ ❖

If *A* is a success in life, then *A* equals *x* plus *y* plus *z*. Work is *x*; *y* is play; and *z* is keeping your mouth shut.

Albert Einstein, *Age Doesn't Matter Unless You're a Cheese*

❖ ❖ ❖

It's not whether you win or lose, but how you place the blame.

John Peers, "1,001 Logical Laws", *The Manager's Book of Quotations*

❖ ❖ ❖

If you had to identify, in one word, the reason why the human race has not achieved and never will achieve, its full potential, that word would be: "meetings."

Davie Barry, "Dave Barry Turns 50", *Graduates Are Special*

❖ ❖ ❖

The best parachute folders are the ones who jump themselves.

Anonymous, *The Manager's Book of Quotations*

❖ ❖ ❖

A paradox is only the truth standing on its head to attract attention.

G.K. Chesterton, *If Ignorance Is Bliss, Why Aren't There More Happy People?*

❖ ❖ ❖

...a sense of humor can be a great help—particularly a sense of humor about (oneself). William Howard Taft joked about his own corpulence and people loved it; took nothing from his inherent dignity. Lincoln eased tense moments with bawdy stories, and often poked fun at himself—and history honors him for this human quality. A sense of humor is part of the art of leadership, of getting along with people, of getting things done."

Dwight D.Eisenhower

❖ ❖ ❖

How Should I Lead and Influence My Team and Organization?

The most dangerous leadership myth is that leaders are born—that there is a genetic factor to leadership. Myth asserts that people simply either have certain charismatic qualities or not. That's nonsense; in fact, the opposite is true.

Leaders are made rather than born. Warren Bennis

❖ ❖ ❖

Leadership is not magnetic personality—that can just as well be a glib tongue. It is not "making friends and influencing people"—that is flattery. Leadership is lifting a person's vision to higher sights, the raising of a person's performance to a higher standard, and the building of a personality beyond its normal limitations.

Peter Drucker

❖ ❖ ❖

Leadership is the capacity to translate vision into reality.

Warren G. Bennis

❖ ❖ ❖

Managers are people who do things right. Leaders are people who do the right thing; The manager accepts the status quo; the leader challenges it.

Warren G. Bennis

❖ ❖ ❖

The manager asks how and when; the leader asks what and why. The manager has a short-range view; the leader has a long-range perspective. The manager has his eye on the bottom line; the leader has his eye on the horizon.

Warren G. Bennis

❖ ❖ ❖

Accountability begins by clearly defining results. When people are held accountable for an unclear result, they feel ambushed, and taken advantage of, rather than empower. The crucial element of personal and organizational accountability should be woven into the very fabric of the business character, process, and culture of organizational life.

Tom Smith

❖ ❖ ❖

What Are The Real Benefits of Working As a Team?

Never doubt that a small group of committed people can change the world.
Indeed, it is the only thing that ever has.

Margaret Mead

❖ ❖ ❖

Everything in the world we want to do or get done,
we must do with and through people.

Earl Nightingale

❖ ❖ ❖

Great things are accomplished by talented people who
believe they will accomplish them.

Warren G. Bennis

❖ ❖ ❖

Talent wins games, but teamwork and intelligence wins championships.

Michael Jordan

❖ ❖ ❖

The strength of the team is each individual member...
the strength of each member is the team.

Phil Jackson

❖ ❖ ❖

Everything you want is just outside your comfort zone.

Robert G. Allen

❖ ❖ ❖

The single defining quality of leaders is their capacity to create and realize a
vision.

Kenneth Blanchard

❖ ❖ ❖

Successful leaders embrace the power of teamwork by tapping
into the innate strengths each person brings to the table.

Scott Beare

❖ ❖ ❖

We all stand on the shoulders of those great men and women who have
gone before us. With gratitude, we give thanks for our abundant freedoms
and blessings that we inherit. How we live our lives and what we
contribute to others in this life, will not only honor our past, but
give great opportunity to the next generation and their future legacy.

Michael K. Simpson

❖ ❖ ❖

I am a member of a team and rely on the team. I defer to it and sacrifice for it,
because the team, not the individual, is the ultimate champion.

Mia Hamm

❖ ❖ ❖

The nice thing about teamwork is that you always have others on your side.

Margaret Carty

❖ ❖ ❖

A team is a group of people who may not be the same in
experience, talent, or education but in commitment.

Patricia Fripp

❖ ❖ ❖

Teamwork is the ability to work together towards a common vision. The ability
to direct individual accomplishment toward organizational objectives.
It is the fuel that allows common people to attain uncommon results.

Andrew Carnegie

❖ ❖ ❖

Those who can command themselves, command others.

William Hazlitt

❖ ❖ ❖

All winning teams are goal-oriented. Teams like these win consistently because everyone connected with them concentrate on specific objectives. They go about their business with blinders on; nothing will distract them from achieving their aims.

Lou Holtz

❖ ❖ ❖

Individual commitment to a group effort—that is what makes a team work, a company work, a society work, a civilization work.

Vince Lombardi

❖ ❖ ❖

Alone we can do so little, together we can do so much.

Helen Keller

❖ ❖ ❖

Coming together is a beginning. Keeping together is a progress. Working together is success.

James Crook

❖ ❖ ❖

In the end, all business operations can be reduced to three words: people, product, and profit. Unless you've got a good team, you can't do much with the other two.

Lee Iacocca

❖ ❖ ❖

You can do what I cannot do. I can do what you cannot do. Together we can do great things.

Mother Teresa

❖ ❖ ❖

Leadership is a matter of having people look at you and gain confidence, seeing how you react. If you're in control, they're in control.

Tom Landry

❖ ❖ ❖

Build for your team a feeling on oneness, of dependence on one another and of strength to be delivered by unity.

Vince Lombardi

❖ ❖ ❖

The key element in the art of working together are how to deal with change and how to deal with conflict...the needs of the team are best met when we meet the needs of individual persons.

Max De Pree

❖ ❖ ❖

A true leader has the confidence to stand alone, the courage to make tough decisions and the compassion to listen to the needs of others.

M.H. McKee

❖ ❖ ❖

When everybody on the team is accountable, the team's effectiveness rises above the sum of its parts. Each team member does not just do what is asked, but what is needed.

John H. Murphy

❖ ❖ ❖

Contrary to popular belief, there most certainly is an "I" in "team." It is the same "I" that appears three times in "responsibility."

Amber Harding

❖ ❖ ❖

Unity is strength...where there is team work and collaboration, wonderful things can be achieved.

Mattie Stepanick

❖ ❖ ❖

Teamwork can be defined in one word—"Complimentary"...meaning, one can organize their team to leverage their strengths and minimize their weaknesses by leveraging the strengths of others.

Stephen R. Covey

❖ ❖ ❖

A hundred thousand men coming one after another could not move a ton of weight, but the united strength of fifty would transport it with ease.

George Washington

❖ ❖ ❖

People acting together as a group can accomplish things which no individual acting alone could ever hope to bring about.

Franklin D. Roosevelt

❖ ❖ ❖

Leadership is getting someone to do what they don't want to do, to achieve what they want to achieve.

Tom Landry

❖ ❖ ❖

How Can a Clear Purpose, Mission, and Vision Provide Us With Focus and Great Success?

Where there is no vision, the people perish.

Proverbs 29:18

❖ ❖ ❖

People with goals succeed because they know where they are going.
It's as simple as that.

Earl Nightingale

❖ ❖ ❖

Our greatest danger in life is in permitting the urgent things to
crowd out the most important.

Charles Hummel

❖ ❖ ❖

The future you see is the future you get.

Robert G. Allen

❖ ❖ ❖

Without a clear mission statement, you may climb to the top of
the ladder and then realize it was leaning against the wrong wall.

Stephen R. Covey

❖ ❖ ❖

The key is not to prioritize what's on your schedule, but to schedule your
priorities.

Stephen Covey

❖ ❖ ❖

We should not be asking the question: What keeps you awake at
night, rather we should ask, what gets you up in the morning?

William Taylor

❖ ❖ ❖

We should be painting a vastly greater mural on a vastly more spacious wall.

John Gardner

❖ ❖ ❖

Many leaders make the mistake of running their business by attention deficit disorder – where everything becomes too shiny and all important. If a leader tries to makes everything urgent and important, then nothing is important. It is critical for leaders' to define what is most strategically important. Then, they will have the capability to say "no" or to say "when" while the temptation comes their way to say "yes" to everything.

Michael K. Simpson

❖ ❖ ❖

If you don't set your goals based upon your Mission Statement, you may be climbing the ladder of success only to realize, when you get to the top of the ladder, you are leaning against the wrong wall.

Stephen R. Covey

❖ ❖ ❖

Management is efficient in climbing the ladder of success; leadership determines whether the ladder is leaning against the right wall.

Stephen R. Covey

❖ ❖ ❖

When you have a mission, you give yourself purpose—and that adds clarity to all actions and decisions that follow. There's an underestimated value of articulating your mission: It focuses you, points you in a new direction, alters your behavior, and as a result, changes other people's perception of you.

Marshall Goldsmith

❖ ❖ ❖

Leadership is the capacity to translate vision into reality.

Warren Bennis

❖ ❖ ❖

If you work just for money, you'll never make it, but if you love what you are doing and you always put the customer first, success will be yours.

Ray Kroc

❖ ❖ ❖

The very essence of leadership is that you have a vision. It's got to be a vision you articulate clearly and forcefully on every occasion.
You can't blow an uncertain trumpet.

Theodore Hesburgh

❖ ❖ ❖

Leaders need to have a bold vision and dreams of their future success, and then, courageously dare to go and get them.

Michael K. Simpson

❖ ❖ ❖

If we don't try, we don't do; and if we don't do, then why are we here?

Shenandoah

❖ ❖ ❖

I try and teach people not to lose sight of what is important and not to be motivated just by money or a job or position, but to see purpose and achievement in ethical and spiritual growth. Our focus is on empowerment through purpose and education. I want to inspire people to reach their true potential and make it to the best versions of themselves. With that structure in place, it is amazing what can be achieved.

Bronco Mendenhall

❖ ❖ ❖

You don't make decisions because they are easy. You don't make decisions because they are cheap. You don't make decisions because they are popular. You make decisions because they are right.

Theodore Hesburgh

❖ ❖ ❖

Life is God's gift to man. What we do with our life is our gift to God.

Harold B. Lee

❖ ❖ ❖

What Are Effective Uses of Power and Influence With Others?

The best leaders are those who ask the best questions.

Rick Warren

❖ ❖ ❖

Great leaders are not those who seek great power, but rather, those who have great power thrust upon them.

Worf, Star Trek DSN

❖ ❖ ❖

A leader is best when people barely know that he exists.

Lao Tzu

❖ ❖ ❖

Perhaps the most central characteristic of authentic leadership is the relinquishing of the impulse to dominate other.

David Cooper

❖ ❖ ❖

A leader leads by example not by force.

Sun Tzu

❖ ❖ ❖

Be good, do good, and always seek to take care of the less fortunate people.

Dennis Haslam

❖ ❖ ❖

None of us is as smart as all of us.

Ken Blanchard

❖ ❖ ❖

People ask the difference between the leader and a boss.
The leader leads and the boss drives.

Theodore Roosevelt

❖ ❖ ❖

You've got to love people more than your position.

John C. Maxwell

❖ ❖ ❖

Giving people a little more than they expect is a good way to get
back a lot more than you'd expect.

Robert Half

❖ ❖ ❖

To lead people, walk behind them.

Lao Tzu

❖ ❖ ❖

A great leader never sets himself above his followers
except in carrying responsibilities.

Jules Ormont

❖ ❖ ❖

A good leader inspires people to have confidence in their leader. A great leader
inspires people to have confidence in themselves.

Lao Tzu

❖ ❖ ❖

A gifted leader is one who is capable of touching your heart.

Jacob Samuel Potofsky

❖ ❖ ❖

Appreciate everything your associates do for the business. Nothing else can quite
substitute for a few well-chosen, well-timed, sincere words of praise.
They are absolutely free and worth a fortune.

Sam Walton

❖ ❖ ❖

If your actions inspire others to dream more, do more, and
become more, you are a leader.

John Quincy Adams

❖ ❖ ❖

Leadership is not about power, position, title, or fame—it is about using your
personal influence to raise-up others abundantly around you.

Michael K. Simpson

❖ ❖ ❖

Everyone wants to fool that the hours they spend at work everyday
matter, so let your team members know the value of their contribution
in making your business a success.

Peter Drucker

❖ ❖ ❖

You can have everything in life that you want if you will just help enough other
people get what they want.

Zig Ziglar

❖ ❖ ❖

Remember, when you were made a leader, you weren't given a crown, you were
given a responsibility to bring out the best in others.

Jack Welch

❖ ❖ ❖

Here is a simple but powerful rule—always give people more
than what they expected to get.

Nelson Boswell

❖ ❖ ❖

The greatest management principle in the world is: "the things that
get rewarded and appreciated get done."

Michael LeBoeuf

❖ ❖ ❖

The best leaders are those who ask the best questions?

Rick Warren

❖ ❖ ❖

They don't care how much you know until they know how much you care.

Theodore Roosevelt

❖ ❖ ❖

Everyone can be great because anybody can serve. You don't have to have a college degree to serve. You don't have to make your subject and your verb agree to serve. You only need a heart full of grace. A soul generated by love.

Martin Luther King, Jr.

❖ ❖ ❖

Great leaders get results in ways that inspire trust with all key stakeholders.

Stephen M. R. Covey

❖ ❖ ❖

"Follow the leader" is more than a game when we remember that the power to lead is the power to mislead, and the power to mislead is the power to destroy.

Thomas S. Monson

❖ ❖ ❖

True leadership must be for the benefit of the followers, not the enrichment of the leaders.

Robert Townsend

❖ ❖ ❖

I count on delegating work to people, trusting them to do the job, and helping them achieve success.

Lakshmi

❖ ❖ ❖

No executive has ever suffered because his subordinates were strong and effective.

Peter Drucker

❖ ❖ ❖

I believe that the people around me are cleverer. Rather than interfering, I count on delegating work, trusting them to do the job, and helping them achieve success.

Lakshmi

❖ ❖ ❖

The man who keeps busy helping the man below him won't have time to envy the man above him.

Henrietta Mears

❖ ❖ ❖

Servanthood begins with personal security. Only those secure with themselves will stoop down and help others. And only the secure will stretch and attempt great undertakings.

John C. Maxwell

❖ ❖ ❖

No person can be a great leader unless he takes genuine joy in the success of those under him.

W.A. Nance

❖ ❖ ❖

You will never become a fine leader, until you become a fine servant.

Ellie Lofaro

❖ ❖ ❖

Self-serving people see what they have as what they own. Serving people see what they have as what's on loan.

John C. Maxwell

❖ ❖ ❖

You will find as you look back upon your life that the moments when you have really lived, are the moments when you have done things in the spirit of love.

Henry Drummond

❖ ❖ ❖

Charity never fails.

1 Corinthians 13:8

❖ ❖ ❖

To love God and your fellowmen rests all the laws of the prophets.

Jesus of Nazareth

❖ ❖ ❖

The love of our neighbor is the only door out of the dungeon of self.

George McDonald

❖ ❖ ❖

While faith makes all things possible, it is love that makes all things easy.

Evan H. Hopkins

❖ ❖ ❖

The supreme happiness of life is the conviction of being loved for yourself, or, more correctly, in spite of yourself.

Victor Hugo

❖ ❖ ❖

I have found the paradox that if I love until it hurts, then there is no more hurt, but only more love.

Mother Teresa

❖ ❖ ❖

Things human must be known to be loved; things divine must be loved to be known.

Blaise Pascal

❖ ❖ ❖

This past year I was diagnosed with cancer and faced the possibility that my life would end sooner that I'd planned. Thankfully, it now looks as if I'll be spared. I have a clear idea of how my ideas had have generated enormous revenue impact for companies that I have consulted in my research. I've concluded that the metric by which God will assess my life isn't dollars but the individual people whose lives we have touched for good. Don't worry about the level of prominence you have achieved; worry about the individuals you have helped to become better people.

Dr. Clayton M. Christensen

❖ ❖ ❖

What Is the Value of Sacrificing Our Immediate Wants Now for Something of Greater Value Later?

The price of greatness is responsibility.

Sir Winston Churchill

❖ ❖ ❖

What is right is often forgotten by what is convenient.

Bodie Thoene

❖ ❖ ❖

We cannot get what we have never had, unless we are willing to do what we have never done.

Brian Tracy

❖ ❖ ❖

You must gain control over your money or the lack of it will forever control you.

Dave Ramsey

❖ ❖ ❖

If you want to accomplish things you've never done before, you'll need to start doing things you've never done before.

Stephen R. Covey

❖ ❖ ❖

Let us have faith that right makes might, and in that faith let us to the end, dare to do our duty as we understand it.

Abraham Lincoln

❖ ❖ ❖

It isn't enough to do one's best. One must do what is necessary.

Sir Winston Churchill

❖ ❖ ❖

One half of knowing what you want, is knowing what you must give up before you get it.

Sidney Howard

❖ ❖ ❖

Nothing of worth or weight can be achieved with half a mind, with a faint heart, and with a lame endeavor.

Isaac Barrow

❖ ❖ ❖

If no changes were necessary for you to achieve financial independence, you'd already be there.

John Cummuta

❖ ❖ ❖

When God measures people, He checks the heart not the head.

John Maxwell

❖ ❖ ❖

Nobody who ever gave his best regretted it.

George Halas

❖ ❖ ❖

How Can We Improve Our Relationships by Affirming, Encouraging, and Complimenting the Worth and Potential in Others?

Carve your name on hearts not on marble.

Charles H. Spurgeon

❖ ❖ ❖

You get the best efforts from others not by lighting a fire beneath them, but by building a fire within.

Bob Nelson

❖ ❖ ❖

No man will make a great leader who wants to do it all himself, or get all the credit for doing it.

Andrew Carnagie

❖ ❖ ❖

Some people say they simply fell out of love. That is wrong. Love is a verb and a choice not just a feeling. We either choose to love or choose not to love. Our choice may be to love a person more than anything they do that bugs us.

Gordon B. Hinckley

❖ ❖ ❖

Leaders don't create more followers, they create more leaders.

Tom Peters

❖ ❖ ❖

The growth and development of people is the highest calling of leadership.

Harvey S. Firestone

❖ ❖ ❖

I will speak ill of no man, and speak all the good I know of everybody.

Benjamin Franklin

❖ ❖ ❖

There is no second chance to make a good first impression.

Benjamin Franklin

❖ ❖ ❖

The first responsibility of a leader is to define reality, the second is to say "Thank you." In between the two, the leader must become a servant.

Max De Pree

❖ ❖ ❖

Encouragement is oxygen to the soul.

George M. Adams

❖ ❖ ❖

Keep away from people who try to belittle your ambitions. Small people always do that, but really great people make you feel that you, too, can become great.

Mark Twain

❖ ❖ ❖

Take the challenge to pay a compliment to at least three different people every day for thirty days and see how it has altered your own outlook on others and on your life. The compliments must be a sincere, honest statement of praise for some objective trait or merit that you have noticed and deserves commendation.

George Crane

❖ ❖ ❖

Do you want to know how to get others to like you? Like them first.

John Maxwell

❖ ❖ ❖

You can't hold a man down without staying down with him.

Booker T. Washington

❖ ❖ ❖

The world is starving for appreciation. It is hungry for compliments. You must start the ball rolling and begin by first noticing and saying nice things to your colleagues and companions. Follow the elevator principles: we can either lift people up, or take them down in our relationships.

George Crane

❖ ❖ ❖

You can't make the other fellow feel important in your presence if
you secretly feel that he is a nobody.

Les Giblin

❖ ❖ ❖

Every man is entitled to be valued by his best moments.

Ralph Waldo Emerson

❖ ❖ ❖

You cannot shake hands with a clenched first.

Indira Gandhi

❖ ❖ ❖

Treat a man as he is and he will remain as he is...Treat a man as he can or should
be and he will become as he can and should be.

Goethe

❖ ❖ ❖

Leaders at their best— provide great vision, purpose, direction, and meaning.
They engage and motive the hearts and minds of all people, at all levels in a way
where they feel valued, appreciated, and respected. Leaders at their worst—fail
to listen, forget to engage others, don't create clarity, and believe that
authoritatively telling people what to do really works.

Michael Simpson

❖ ❖ ❖

The purpose in life is not to win or beat others. The purpose of life is to grow and
to share. When you come to look back on all that you have done in life, you will
get more satisfaction from the pleasure you have brought into other people's
lives than you will from the times that you outdid and defeated them.

Harold Kushner

❖ ❖ ❖

Remember the names of people you meet, you will
make a great second impression.

John Maxwell

❖ ❖ ❖

All effective leaders possess emotional intelligence. For star performance in all jobs, in every field, emotional competence is two times (2x) as important as purely cognitive abilities. For success at the highest levels, in leadership positions, emotional competence accounts for virtually the entire advantage... Given that emotional competencies make up two-thirds (2/3) or more of the ingredients of star performers, the data suggest that finding people who have these abilities, or nurturing them in existing employees, adds tremendous value to an organization's bottom line. But how much? In simple jobs like machine operators or clerks, those in the top one-percent (1%) with emotional competency were three times (3x) more productive (by value). For jobs of medium complexity, like sales clerks, or mechanics, a single top emotional competent person was twelve times (12x) more productive (by value).

Daniel Goleman

❖ ❖ ❖

Coach Paul "Bear" Bryant would say he was just a plow hand from Arkansas. But his wisdom and ability to encourage others helped him build some of the best football teams of all time. His teams were held together by three key things that he would say: 1. If anything goes bad—I did it. 2. If anything goes semi-good— then we did it. 3. If anything goes real good—then you did it.

Everything in the world we want to do or get done, we must do with and through people.

Earl Nightingale

❖ ❖ ❖

The secret to encouraging others is to get excited about the right things. Some people get excited about pointing out mistakes or finding someone's failure. Instead we should get excited about their strengths and the little things they are doing right.

John C. Maxwell

❖ ❖ ❖

Anyone can be a management hack, that goes around finding fault, blaming others, pointing fingers, making excuses, and influencing others with fear and intimidation. But not everyone is leader. Leaders are very good at catching people doing things right, are abundant with honest praise, celebrates the successes others, and helps raise up people around them.

Michael K. Simpson

❖ ❖ ❖

People are lonely because they build wall instead of bridges.

Joseph F. Newton

❖ ❖ ❖

The best way to cheer yourself up is to cheer everybody else up.

Mark Twain

❖ ❖ ❖

Flatter me, and I may not believe you. Criticize me, and I may not like you.
Ignore me, and I may not forgive you. Encourage me, and I will not forget you.

William A. Ward

❖ ❖ ❖

I have never seen a man who could do real work except under the stimulus of
encouragement and the enthusiasm, and the approval of the people for whom he
is working.

Charles Schwab

❖ ❖ ❖

Correction does much, but encouragement does more; encouragement after
censure is the sun after the shower.

Johann Wolfgang Von Goethe

❖ ❖ ❖

A great baseball manager has a knack for making ballplayers think they are
better than they really are. He forces you to have a good opinion of yourself. And
once you learn how good you really are, you never settle for playing anything less
than your very best.

Reggie Jackson

❖ ❖ ❖

Effective leadership requires the achievement of business results in the right way
— without demeaning, demoralizing, or destroying people.

Michael Feiner

❖ ❖ ❖

Why Are The Skill and Capacity of Communication, Listening, and Mutual Understanding Critical for Any Great Relationship?

There is nothing noble in feeling superior to some other person.
The true nobility is in being superior to your previous self.

Hindu Proverb

❖ ❖ ❖

Being able to put aside one's self-centered focus and impulses has social benefits: it opens the way to empathy, to real listening, to taking another person's perspective. Empathy, as we have seen, leads to caring, altruism, and compassion. Seeing things from another's perspective breaks down biased stereotypes, and so breeds tolerance and acceptance of differences.

Daniel Goleman

❖ ❖ ❖

Reading emotions through empathy helps to receive another person's perspectives, improve sensitivity to others feelings, and able to listen from others' frame of reference.

Daniel Goleman

❖ ❖ ❖

Big people monopolize the listening. Small people monopolize the talking.

David Schwartz

❖ ❖ ❖

One of the best ways to persuade others is with your ears—by listening to them.

Dean Rusk

❖ ❖ ❖

Listen to the whisper and you won't have to hear the screams.

Cherokee Saying

❖ ❖ ❖

They may not remember all that I say. But they will never forget the way I made them feel.

Carl W. Buechner

❖ ❖ ❖

The best leaders…almost without exception and at every level, are master users of stories and symbols.

Tom Peters

❖ ❖ ❖

Unexpressed feelings never die; they are buried alive and come forth in uglier ways.

Stephen R. Covey

❖ ❖ ❖

The exact words that you use are far less important than the energy, intensity, and conviction with which you use them.

Jules Rose

❖ ❖ ❖

Most people listen not with the intent to understand, but with the intent to reply.

Stephen R. Covey

❖ ❖ ❖

The greatest gift you can give another is the purity of your attention.

Richard Moss

❖ ❖ ❖

Listening, not imitation, may be the sincerest form of flattery.

Joyce Brothers

❖ ❖ ❖

To be with another empathically means that for the time being, you lay aside your own views and values in order to enter another's world without prejudice. In a sense you lay aside yourself; this can only be done by people that are secure in themselves.

Carl Rogers

❖ ❖ ❖

Leadership is not about what leaders say that is important, it is what people hear.

Marshall Goldsmith

❖ ❖ ❖

The most important thing in communication is to hear what isn't being said.

Peter Drucker

❖ ❖ ❖

Genius is the ability to reduce the complicated to the simple.

C. W. Ceran

❖ ❖ ❖

The greatest truths are the simplest—so are the greatest men and women.

Julius Charles Hare

❖ ❖ ❖

Real communication happens when people feel safe.

Ken Blanchard

❖ ❖ ❖

The void created by the failure to communicate is soon filled
with poison, drivel, and misrepresentation.

C. Northcote Parkinson

❖ ❖ ❖

How well we communicate is determined not by how well we
say things but by how well we are understood.

Andrew S. Grove

❖ ❖ ❖

Think like a wise man but communicate in the language of the people.

William Butler Yeats

❖ ❖ ❖

Have an understanding so you don't have a misunderstanding.

Charles Blair

❖ ❖ ❖

If I had to name a single, all-purpose instrument of leadership, it would be communication.

John W. Gardner

❖ ❖ ❖

When I am getting ready to reason with a man, I spend one-third of my time thinking about myself and what I am going to say, and two-thirds thinking about him and what he is going to say.

Abraham Lincoln

❖ ❖ ❖

Illustrations

Planning and preparation are keys to success. Chesley B. "Sully" Sullenberger, III, quickly considered his options, and it was apparent that he would not be able to glide the aircraft to an airport runway. Clear-mindedly, he navigated the heavy craft toward the Hudson River and advised his passengers to "brace for impact." There, using skills he had gained over many years of flying, gliding, and as a safety consultant, Sully safely ditched into the freezing Hudson River. As passengers quickly exited onto the wings of the aircraft, Sully twice went through the cabin to ensure that nobody was left behind. All of the passengers and flight crew were evacuated safely. One week later, the Guild of Air Pilots and Air Navigators honored the entire crew of Flight 1549 with a Masters Medal, for safely executing the emergency ditching and evacuation with no loss of lives . . . a "heroic and unique aviation achievement."

Was this a miracle? . . . Or was it simply the expected outcome following the best preparation? Was it a miracle that first responders from the New York Fire Department, New York Police Department and ferries from the Port Authority were on the scene in just minutes? Or had they anticipated just such an emergency, planned and drilled for the response, and knew exactly what to do in the moment it was required of them?

Author unknown

❖ ❖ ❖

Turkish wrestler Yousouf Ishmaelo came to the United States in 1897 and competed against the Greco-Roman champion Ernest Roeber, and others. Not trusting the currencies of the day, he converted all his winnings into gold coins. He kept these coins—day and night in a belt around his waist. Returning across the Atlantic Ocean, his cruise ship collided with a British vessel and began to sink. Ishmaelo refused to discard his money belt, and he ended up in the water with heavy gold coins around his waist. Although he was a good swimmer, the coins made it impossible for him to stay afloat. He sank to his death at the bottom of the ocean. He sacrificed his most important thing—his life. Money, which was of value, ultimately led to his demise because he could not part from it. Certainly, Ishmaelo's life was more important than his gold coins, but he refused to recognize it and adjust to the circumstances he faced. Just as these valuable gold coins truly contributed to his death, so, too, can valuable goals distract an individual or a team from achieving goals that may be much more important.

Michael Fred Phelps, aka "Flying Fish", became a household name throughout the world in the recently concluded Beijing Olympic Games. His record-eight gold medals in Beijing, combined with 6 gold and 2 bronze medals in Athens four years ago, make him perhaps the greatest Olympian of all time. In the years leading up to this great accomplishment, Phelps had already reached some incredible milestones: he became the youngest male swimmer ever to set a world record at the age of 15 years and nine months, he had won 17 World

Championships between 2001 and 2007, and he was the World Swimmer of the Year in 2003, 2004 and 2006. Even with all of this recognition, Phelps' most significant prize was winning his FIRST gold medal in Athens in 2004. As the media and other swimmers were surrounding to congratulate him, he could only think of getting to his biggest supporter: his mother, Debbie Phelps. He quickly sent her a text message and asked her to meet him at the fence under the grandstand. As he approached her, with great pride and a sense of accomplishment, he held up his gold medal and yelled, "Mom, look what I've done!"

Author unknown

❖ ❖ ❖

Growing the Seeds of Greatness

In these pages you find more advice than you could master in several lifetimes.

Furthermore, some advice conflicts with others. Should you be bold or compassionate, stand your ground or cooperate, seize the moment or be patient?

Together, the abundance of good counsel and its inconsistency draw attention to some truths that we now want to enunciate.

Wisdom requires choice, personal responsibility, and accountability.

When we say that you already have the seeds of greatness in you, we mean that you know better than anyone else what you most need to progress. The questions around which the quotations are organized are designed to get you thinking, "What do I need most? Where am I on my journey Do I have clear purpose and clarity? How am I showing up as a leader? How can I become the person I want to be?"

As you think about the questions and the good counsel contained in each book section, you will be naturally drawn to some questions over others. It will probably require some clear-headed thinking (maybe even a consultation or advice with a trusted friend) to make sure you emphasize what you most need, but no one can make that decision better than you. No one has ever lived your life before, and to live it well, you need to choose where to focus your attention and your efforts

And for all the voices of good counsel you find here, no one but you is responsible for what you become. Drinking deeply in fountains of timeless wisdom should convince you that people are thoroughly responsible for who and what they are, now and in the future. When a different day dawns, though, when you fully believe that these basic truths apply to you, too—when you decide that you can change, that you can grow the seeds of greatness that are already within, and thereby effectively impact your future for good and that of the people about which you care the most.

Which brings us to a paradox. Those who discover the principles of making good choices, complete personal responsibility and accountability also influence others the most. How can that be? Because people who have learned how to truly be responsible for their attitudes, happiness, choices, and actions attract those who haven't so learned. It's natural. Such people, having not yet accepted 100% personal responsibility, are looking for people to ignite and unleash this personal power that lie within them.

Leadership is a choice! May your seeds of greatness sprout, grow, bless your life, and trigger change in others.

Best of happiness and success on your journey!

Michael K. Simpson

About the Author

For over 25 years, Michael's practical, real world, business experience has been in corporate leadership, executive development, executive coaching, advisory and consulting services, sales and marketing, and business development.

Michael is the Global Director for FranklinCovey - Columbia University's Executive Coaching Certification Program. He is a Senior Consultant in FranklinCovey's Leadership, Strategy Execution, and Trust Practices. He is an executive coach to many of the world's top leaders from Fortune 50 companies.

Mr. Simpson was on faculty for three years instructing senior executives with the late Dr. Stephen R. Covey and Dr. Ram Charan at FranklinCovey's Executive Leadership Summit held at Deer Valley and Sundance, Utah ski resorts.

Michael is the co-author of several leadership and coaching books and articles, including: Ready, Aim, Excel with Dr. Marshall Goldsmith and Dr. Ken Blanchard. Unlocking Potential: 7 Coaching Skills That Transform Individuals, Teams, and Organizations. Your Seeds of Greatness: The World's Greatest Leadership Quote Books with Dr. David Paxman. Talent Unleashed: How to Conduct 3 Essential Leadership Conversations with A. Roger Merrill, Shawn Moon, and Todd Davis. The Execution-focused Leader with PricewaterhouseCoopers Advisory Group. Coaching Team and Organizational Trust with Stephen M.R. Covey

Formerly, Mr. Simpson was a Principal Consultant for the global management consulting firm, Pricewaterhouse-Cooper's (PwC) in their Strategic and Organizational Change Practice in New York City, NY. Michael has held executive management positions' for two leading technology companies as Vice President of Sales and Marketing and Vice President of Business Development.

For over 18 years at FranklinCovey, Michael has delivered, advised, and coached some of the world's top leaders and teams in leadership, strategy execution, and talent management. He has certified and coached executives throughout the United States, Canada, China, India, Singapore, Malaysia, Indonesia, Philippines, Thailand, Vietnam, Mexico, Central and South America, Brazil, Great Britain, Germany, Iceland, Norway, Sweden, Finland, Denmark, Belgium, Holland, Russia, Egypt, and Saudi Arabia.

In 1995-96, Michael was an External Consultant at Nike in Guangzhou, China. He designed and developed a year-long 'leadership program' for Chinese hi potential managers. This course was rated as the #1 management development program at Nike. Michael was voted by the Chinese Government's Guangdong's Commission of Education as one of the top 10 professors among 150 foreign teachers at South China's University of Technology in Guangzhou. He is an Adjunct Professor at Columbia College's School of Business Administration and has taught classes in Organizational Behavior and Leadership for BYU's Marriott School of Management.

Mr. Simpson's clients include: Marriott, Frito-Lay, John Deere, Lilly, GE Capital, TE Connectivity, ExxonMobil, Nike, Procter & Gamble, Johnson & Johnson, Unilever, Coca-Cola, Chiquita Brands, PricewaterhouseCoopers, Ernst & Young, Atlanta Falcons, Orlando Magic, Tafe India, Elanco, Hewlett Packard-EDS, Xerox-ACS, Juniper Networks, Ericsson, Honeywell, Microsoft, IBM, Samsung-Canada, Amway, H&R Block, Fairview Ridges Hospital, Loma Linda Hospital, Abbvie Pharmaceuticals, Alvogen Pharmaceuticals Iceland, Truven Health, Highmark Health Services, Cox Communications, Intel, Nokia Finland, Motorola, Verizon, Maxis Malaysia, Mobily-Saudi Arabia, Cummins Engine, HSBC Bank, Central Bank Philippines, Central Bank Thailand, Huntington Bank, Affin Bank, Marafiq Saudi Arabia, Kuwait Finance, Iskandar Malaysia, Prudential BSN, ING Insurance, New York Life, Farmers Insurance, 21st Century Insurance, Kimpton Hotels, Darden Restaurants, Kroger's, Associated Foods, NCH Corporation, Goodyear, Payless Shoes, IC Company Denmark, Lockheed-Martin, Honeywell, Westinghouse, Malaysia Rubber Board, Southern California Edison, NY State Workers Compensation Fund, Iowa State Workforce Development, GA Dept. of Human Resources, GA Technology Authority, U.S. EPA, U.S. Army Corp of Engineers, Los Alamos Nat'l Laboratory, U.S. Nuclear Regulatory Commission, U.S. Dept. of Defense, U.S. Defense Intelligence Agency, LA Unified School District, Orange County CA School District, Alamo Colleges TX.

Michael has a master's degree in Organizational Behavior from Columbia University and a bachelor's degree in International Relations from Brigham Young University. Michael and his wife Cynthia live near the beautiful Wasatch Mountains of Utah with their four boys: Zachary, Luke, Jacob, and McKay. He enjoys traveling, snow skiing, mountain biking, tennis, and golf. For over 25 years, Michael's practical, real world, business experience has been in corporate leadership, executive development, executive coaching, advisory and consulting services, sales and marketing, and business development.

Simpson Executive Coaching

Michael is an internationally sought after executive coach, leadership consultant, keynote speaker, and distinguished author who has published seven books and several whitepapers in the areas of coaching, leadership and management development, change management, and organizational behavior.

If you want to get in touch with Michael for Coaching or Keynote visit:

http://www.simpsonexecutivecoaching.com/

or email Michael at:

msimpson@ebacs.net

Juxtabook Publishing

juxtabook

If you would like to Self-Publish your book contact Juxtabook for a quote. eBook, Print on Demand, and Marketing services offered.

Visit:

www.juxtabook.com or email us at support@juxtabook.com